MW00878790

LETTERS TO MY

LEGACY

By Ryan Grage

Official Book #1

More to come...

Dedication

To the community that allowed me to share my passion and knowledge of fitness—thank you for trusting me and putting in the work. Together, we built more than just strength; we forged resilience and dedication. This book is for those who showed up, pushed through, and embraced the journey. Here's to the legacy we created one rep at a time.

Chapter 1: On Leading by Example

Legacy of Integrity: A Conversation with My Children, Grandchildren, and All Those Seeking Inspiration

Introduction

Children, grandchildren, and all those who seek inspiration, gather around. I want to share something deeply personal with you—something that has guided my every step and shaped the person I am today. It's about leading by example, a legacy I hope to pass down to you and inspire others along the way.

Paul Walker once said, "If one day the speed kills me, do not cry because I was smiling." This quote beautifully encapsulates the joy and passion one finds in living life to the fullest. It's this kind of passion and commitment that I want to share with you, a dedication to living with purpose and integrity.

Leading by Example in Everyday Life

Every morning, before the sun rises, I engage in bodyweight functional fitness, biking, or rowing. I choose one or two small exercises to get my body ready and awake for the day. I work up a good sweat because sweating is good for the soul. It keeps the demons at bay for the moment. It's not just about fitness; it's about discipline. Your actions speak louder than words, and I've always believed in showing, not just telling, the importance of hard work and resilience. When you see me wake up early, make healthy meal choices, and treat everyone with respect, I hope you understand that these actions are not just for me, but for you—to show you the way.

Leading by example means embodying the values we hold dear. It's easy to talk about integrity, but it's our actions that define us. I've always aimed to demonstrate that success comes from relentless effort and dedication.

Marcus Aurelius once said, "Waste no more time arguing about what a good man should be. Be one." Integrity isn't just a concept to discuss; it's a way of life. Leading by example means embodying honesty, resilience, and compassion. These are the virtues I strive to instill in you.

Philosophical Insights and Practical Lessons

Life is full of opportunities, and every day is a chance to prepare for them. By leading through action, I've aimed to demonstrate the importance of being ready and embracing every opportunity with both hands. Here are some practical steps to lead by example:

1. **Set Clear Goals**: Know what you want to achieve and work towards it every day. Write down your goals, revisit them often, and adjust as needed. Don't forget, you will need to learn the difference between an excuse and the need to give yourself grace.
2. **Practice What You Preach**: Live your values. If you believe in kindness, be kind. If you value hard work, work hard. It doesn't come easy, I promise!
3. **Maintain Consistency**: Consistency is key. It's the small, daily actions that build character and lead to greatness. Stick with it.

These principles not only serve as guiding lights on your journey but also represent the essence of determination, integrity, and resilience needed to achieve true greatness.

As Grandpa Weber always said, "Regularity will make you and regularity will break you. Simply put, if you regularly suck at life, life will suck." Take these lessons to heart, and you'll not only shape your destiny but inspire those around you.

From the Heart: A Personal Reflection

Leading by example hasn't always been easy. Growing up in an ultra-conservative Christian religion, I was encouraged not to advance my schooling past high school and to dedicate all my free time to the religion. We were also told the world was going to end around the millennium. I'm glad they were wrong. The reason I strive to show that success comes from relentless effort directly stems from this upbringing. I wanted to break free from those constraints and prove that hard work and determination—success through a strong work ethic—could lead to a better life.

Living through the market crash in 2008, the year my daughter London was born, watching my sales and management career go down the drain due to the poor economy, and working in a corn processing plant to pay the bills—all of these experiences taught me resilience. At the corn processing plant, I worked in the boiler house, turbine operations, and feed division; eventually finishing my career in the alcohol division.

The turning point came with a horrific industrial accident in the alcohol division. I was engulfed in flames during an explosion, suffering severe burns that required immediate medical intervention. I was life-flighted to the Iowa City University burn unit for surgery. The physical pain was excruciating, but the emotional and psychological scars ran even deeper.

Surviving the accident left me with PTSD, a constant reminder of the fragility of life and the dangers of the workplace. The incident forced me to confront my fears and reevaluate my priorities. Despite the financial constraints it imposed on my family, I knew I couldn't return to the plant. The trauma was too significant, and continuing in that environment would have jeopardized my mental health and well-being.

This near-death experience became a catalyst for change. As I lay in the hospital bed, reflecting on my life, I realized that I needed to take control of my destiny. I couldn't let the accident define me or hold me back. I made a promise to myself that I would escape the cycle of pain and fear. I decided to channel my energy into something positive—teaching others about fitness and the profound impact it could have on their lives.

Despite my resolve to move forward, the company terminated my employment due to attendance issues. They refused to accept my medical time off, hiding behind legal jargon to justify their actions. This was a devastating blow, but it only strengthened my determination to succeed on my own terms.

The financial uncertainty was daunting, but the desire to make a difference was stronger. I wanted to inspire others to overcome their own challenges and discover the transformative power of fitness. You may never know who you inspire, but I promise you it is worth the effort.

Through these challenges, I've learned the true meaning of perseverance. Every time I tucked my kids in bed at night, I knew I had to keep going. The moment you give up is the moment you let someone else win. I couldn't let you see me give up. Perseverance, even in the face of adversity, is what defines us.

Embracing Diversity and Celebrating Strengths

Each of you is unique, with your own strengths and personalities. I've always tried to embrace and celebrate your individuality. Love knows no bounds, whether you're my biological child or adopted. Celebrate your unique strengths and use them to contribute to the family's unity and success.

"We are all part of a larger whole. And the whole requires our contribution." By embracing diversity within our family, we strengthen the bonds that hold us together. This diversity is our strength, and it's something I'm immensely proud of.

A Legacy of Love and Discipline

Balancing love and discipline have been one of the most important aspects of my parenting. I've shown you unconditional love while also setting clear boundaries. As Marcus Aurelius reminds us, "Do the right thing right now. Because the right thing at the wrong time is the wrong thing." This balance is crucial. It teaches respect, responsibility, and the importance of making the right choices.

Fostering Resilience and Independence

Resilience and independence are traits I've always valued and tried to instill in you. Life will throw challenges your way, and it's important to face them head-on. Encourage risk-taking and learn from your mistakes. "Failure shows us the way—by showing us what isn't the way." Embrace failure as a steppingstone to growth.

Nurturing Emotional Intelligence

Creating a safe environment for emotional expression is vital. To be calm is the highest achievement of the self. Teach yourself to manage emotions healthily, modeling empathy and compassion. These are the pillars of emotional intelligence and are crucial for navigating life's complexities and building meaningful relationships.

The Power of Presence

Be present in your lives. Engage, listen, share experiences. "Wherever you are, whatever you're doing, act with purpose." This presence builds a foundation of trust and connection. It's a gift that strengthens bonds and fosters a sense of security. Never underestimate the power of being truly present for those you love.

Instilling a Love for Learning

Foster curiosity and a love for learning through diverse experiences. "Education is freedom." Nurture your passion for discovery and knowledge. Encourage questions, explore new interests, and pursue your passions. This will lead to a lifetime of growth and fulfillment.

Celebrating Achievements and Effort

Celebrate both big and small achievements. "Courage isn't an absence of fear. Courage is a triumph over fear." Recognize efforts and hard work, teaching the value of perseverance. Celebrating achievements motivates and inspires continued growth.

Building a Legacy of Values

Shape a legacy of honesty, respect, humility, and compassion. "Ego is the enemy of what you want and of what you have: Of mastering a craft. Of real creative insight. Of working well with others. Of building loyalty and support." These values will guide you through life's complexities. Hold on to them tightly.

The Joy of Parenthood

Amidst challenges, find joy in the journey of parenthood. "Happiness is the pursuit, not the destination." Cherish laughter, milestones, and simple joys together. Parenthood is a journey filled with moments of joy, growth, and discovery.

Conclusion: A Legacy of Love, Strength, and Integrity

My dear children, grandchildren, and all those seeking inspiration, leading by example is not just about what you do but who you are. It's about living your values every day and inspiring others to do the same. As you go through life, remember the lessons we've shared. Embrace the wisdom of the Stoics, the inspiration from modern motivators, and the experiences we've had together.

As Marcus Aurelius said, "Live a good life. If there are gods and they are just, then they will not care how devout you have been but will welcome you based on the virtues you have lived by. If there are gods, but unjust, then you should not want to worship them. If there are no gods, then you will be gone, but will have lived a noble life that will live on in the memories of your loved ones."

Lead by example, live with integrity, and create a legacy that will inspire future generations. This is my hope for you, my legacy, my love.

With all my heart,

Ryan Grage

Chapter 2: On Embracing Diversity in the Family

Legacy of Strength: Celebrating Uniqueness and Unity

Introduction

Family, friends, and all who seek inspiration, gather around. Today, I want to talk about something incredibly important—embracing diversity within our family. Each of you brings something unique to our lives, and it's these differences that make us stronger. This chapter is about celebrating those differences and understanding the power of unity. As we experienced vacationing and eventually living in Florida, our family's strength lies not just in our shared moments, but in our unique individualities coming together.

Understanding and Celebrating Diversity

Every single one of you has strengths and qualities that make you unique. Your individuality is your superpower. Whether it's the resilience of my adopted daughter, Makenna, the intellectual curiosity of my son, Landon, the creative spark of my youngest, Gunnar, or the innate ability to read and manage the energy in the room like my daughter, London—these traits are what make our family dynamic and strong. Embracing these differences isn't just about acceptance; it's about celebrating the richness they bring to our lives.

Diversity in our family means recognizing and valuing these unique qualities. Seneca once said, "We are more often frightened than hurt; and we suffer more from imagination than from reality." To truly embrace diversity, we must let go of our fears and prejudices. We must accept the reality that we are all different and that's not just okay—it's something to be celebrated.

Philosophical Insights

Epictetus taught us, "We are all part of a larger whole. And the whole requires our contribution." This philosophy reminds us that every person, with their unique traits and perspectives, contributes to the greater good of the family and society. By embracing diversity, we not only accept each other's differences but also learn from them, growing stronger together.

I believe in the power of unity through diversity. "Each of us is a piece of a grand puzzle. Only by appreciating each unique piece can we complete the picture." This idea is crucial in understanding that our family's strength comes from our collective differences.

As Dom Toretto famously said, "I don't have friends, I got family." Our family is always willing to stand up alongside those that are family. Be confident in who you are. Your uniqueness will be your strength.

Actionable Advice

Celebrate Individual Strengths: Encourage each other's passions and interests. If one of you loves painting, support them by providing the tools and space to create. If another enjoys sports, cheer them on in every game or match. Your support and encouragement will help each other grow and flourish.

Promote Open Communication: Talk about your differences openly. Have family discussions where everyone can share their thoughts and feelings without judgment. This will foster an environment of trust and understanding. Open communication helps us appreciate where each person is coming from and builds stronger bonds.

Create Inclusive Traditions: Establish family traditions that celebrate diversity. Whether it's cooking a meal from a different culture every month, having a talent show where everyone can showcase their skills, or planning trips that expose us to new experiences and perspectives, these traditions will highlight and honor each person's unique contributions.

Learn from Each Other: Take the time to learn about each other's interests and perspectives. This not only enriches your understanding but also strengthens your bond as a family. Remember, every person you meet knows something you don't. In our family, every member has a lesson to teach and a story to share.

Personal Reflections

Growing up as a Jehovah's Witness wasn't just about living under the weight of religious expectations; it was about navigating the complex social dynamics that came with it. I was one of the better athletes in my school, yet because I wasn't allowed to play sports outside of church-approved activities, I was often mocked for not participating in the very things I excelled at. On top of that, the restrictions on dating led to being called names that no one should ever have to hear, all because I couldn't date girls that didn't share my faith. It was rough, no doubt, but it also shaped me in ways I couldn't appreciate at the time. It taught me that self-worth isn't defined by others' opinions or the labels they try to stick on you. Instead, it comes from knowing who you are and being comfortable in your own skin, regardless of what the world has to say.

A Legacy of Love and Unity

Our family's strength lies in its diversity. Just as Marcus Aurelius said, "The soul becomes dyed with the color of its thoughts," our family is colored with the rich hues of each member's individuality. This diversity is our strength, our foundation, and our legacy.

Eric Thomas once said, "When you want to succeed as bad as you want to breathe, then you'll be successful." Success in our family isn't just about individual achievements but about thriving together, supporting each other, and celebrating our unique strengths. We are a family that understands that true success is measured by our ability to uplift one another. When we crave success with the same intensity we crave air, we harness the unstoppable force within us to achieve greatness together.

Embracing Challenges Together

Life will throw challenges your way, and it's our diverse perspectives that will help us navigate these obstacles. Whether it's facing prejudice, overcoming personal struggles, or supporting each other in times of need, our unity will be our guiding light.

Ryan Holiday, interpreting Marcus Aurelius, said, "The obstacle in the path becomes the path. Never forget, within every obstacle is an opportunity to improve our condition." Simply put, "The Obstacle is the Way." Our diversity allows us to approach problems from different angles, finding solutions that we might not see alone. Each challenge we face together strengthens our bond and prepares us for whatever comes next.

Conclusion: A Legacy of Embracing Diversity

My dear family and friends, as you go through life, remember to embrace and celebrate your differences. Our family's diversity is our strength. By supporting each other and honoring each person's unique contributions, we create a legacy of love, unity, and strength.

I was gifted the quote, "The Man in the Arena," by my manger during a long project. Theodore Roosevelt said in "It is not the critic who counts; not the man who points out how the strong man stumbles, or where the doer of deeds could have done them better. The credit belongs to the man who is actually in the arena, whose face is marred by dust and sweat and blood; who strives valiantly; who errs, who comes short again and again, because there is no effort without error and shortcoming; but who does actually strive to do the deeds; who knows great enthusiasms, the great devotions; who spends himself in a worthy cause; who at the best knows in the end the triumph of high achievement, and who at the worst, if he fails, at least fails while daring greatly, so that his place shall never be with those cold and timid souls who neither know victory nor defeat."

Embrace each other, cherish your unique qualities, and continue to build a family that thrives on diversity and unity.

This is our legacy. This is our strength. This is the Grage way.

With all my love,
Ryan Grage

Chapter 3: The Flame That Burns Within

Introduction: Legacy of Fun and Embracing Authenticity

Mi Famila. Life isn't just about the serious moments; it's also about embracing your fun, eccentric, and quirky side. Today, I want to share with you the importance of being unapologetically yourself and enjoying every bit of it. Embracing your unique traits, no matter how unconventional they may seem, is a vital part of living a fulfilled and authentic life.

The Marvel and DC Connection

Growing up, I was always fascinated by superheroes. Marvel characters like Thor and Iron Man were not just fictional heroes to me; they represented strength, resilience, and the courage to be different. During my CrossFit Port Byron days, with my long hair flowing like Thor and the sharp, innovative mindset of Iron Man, I embraced my inner superhero. It was a time of immense physical strength and intellectual creativity, embracing my unique personality and capabilities.

Thor once said, "I choose to run towards my problems and not away from them. Because that's what heroes do." This quote reminded me to face challenges head-on, while staying true to who I am. Similarly, Iron Man, with his unyielding drive and innovative spirit, taught me that creativity and intelligence are as important as physical strength. Tony Stark's resilience and resourcefulness have always inspired me to push beyond my limits.

But it wasn't just Marvel heroes that fueled my passion. DC Comics' Aqua Man also played a significant role. Dressing up as him for Halloween, I channeled the king of Atlantis' strength and determination. Aqua Man's command over the seas and his unwavering resolve, pierced straight through me, reminding me that true power often lies beneath the surface, waiting to be unleashed.

Philosophical Insights

Embracing your eccentric and quirky side is not just about enjoying comics or movies; it's about celebrating what makes you unique. David Goggins, a modern-day warrior, once said, "You are in danger of living a life so comfortable and soft, that you will die without ever realizing your true potential." Your interests, no matter how unconventional, are part of what makes you, you. They push you out of your comfort zone and help you discover your true potential.

Seneca taught us, "It is the power of the mind to be unconquerable." This means being confident in your quirks and passions, no matter what others think. It's about having the strength to be different and the courage to stand out.

Marcus Aurelius also said in his Meditations, "Don't waste the rest of your time here worrying about other people- unless it affects the common good. It will keep you from doing anything useful. You'll be too preoccupied with what so-and-so is doing, and why, and what they're saying, and what they're thinking, and what they're up to, and all the other things that throw you off and keep you from focusing on your own mind." This profound wisdom reminds us to focus on our path and passions, not to be distracted by the noise of others.

Practical Tips for Embracing Your Quirky Side

- **Celebrate Your Interests**: Dive into your passions with unbridled enthusiasm. Whether it's superheroes, sci-fi, or something else, let your interests shine brightly. These interests are part of the tapestry of your life, adding color and vibrancy. By celebrating what you love, you not only enrich your own life but also inspire those around you to embrace their passions.
- **Find Your Tribe**: Surround yourself with people who share your interests or who appreciate your quirks. Community and support

are essential in embracing who you truly are. Finding your tribe means finding people who understand and accept you, people who uplift you and encourage you to be your best self.

- **Be Authentic**: Authenticity is about being true to yourself. Don't hide your quirks; let them shine. This authenticity will attract genuine connections and enrich your life. In a world where many wears masks, being authentic is a breath of fresh air. It shows strength of character and an unwavering commitment to being true to oneself.
- **Use Your Passions as Strength**: Channel your interests into something productive. For me, it was about incorporating the strength and determination of superheroes into my fitness journey. Your passions can be a source of immense strength, guiding you through challenges and helping you achieve your goals. They can be the fuel that drives you forward, no matter what obstacles you face.

A Fun Journey: The Marvel and DC Universe

Remember when I dressed up as Thor, Hulk, and Aquaman for Halloween? Or when we had Marvel and DC movie marathons? Those were some of the best times, not just because of the fun we had, but because they allowed us to bond over shared interests. These moments are precious and show the power of embracing our inner eccentricities. One of my favorite marvel moments is watching **End Game** in the theaters, with my son Landon. My allergies were really "bothering" me that day. That may have been the moment I realized that dads eventually pass on.

Images and Reflections

Look up Ryan Grage online—whether on social media, Google, or YouTube—and you'll find pieces of my journey. You'll see images from different stages: MMA, CrossFit, weightlifting, and maybe even a bit of powerlifting. Social media wasn't big during my powerlifting era, so those images are rare, but they exist. What you find isn't just about sports. It's about Ryan Grage. Weightlifter. CrossFitter. Powerlifter. These images tell a story of transformation—my evolution. They reflect the raw process of embracing who I am. It's a journey of self-discovery, captured in real time, and the pride of being unapologetically me.

I vividly recall the video on Facebook of me fighting a big, strong opponent at the Davenport Fairgrounds. That fight wasn't just about physical strength but about mental fortitude and respect. No disrespect to my opponent, but that moment showed the power of embracing my unique strengths and the drive to push beyond limits. I didn't back down! I stayed true to myself and kept pushing forward.

The Fight

He was a very muscular and lean man, boasting about his cardio and how he ran 7-10 miles with a weighted vest every day. I believed him 100%. I knew I had to take the fight to him early and wear him down, looking for a first-round knockout. I couldn't let him take me into the deep rounds. I had the strength to push the pace early. As he threw a huge right cross that missed me by a mile, I shot the perfect double leg takedown, carrying him across the ring before slamming him to the ground. I was in full mount, raining down a hailstorm of punches, elbows, and forearms. He didn't go out; he stared right back at me. He finally rolled me because I got out of position, and I quickly found my way to side mount.

I can still hear the voice of my then-girlfriend, you know her as Mom, Amber Grage, screaming louder than anyone in the crowd. My Uncle Bob was the second loudest, screaming "Go Ryan!" My opponent held my gloves, trapping me for a second. He rolled to my guard, and I had a tight guillotine choke on. He tapped, but on the side the ref couldn't see. I let go like all good fighters should do, and he started fighting again. I looked at the ref and said he tapped, but he told us to continue. My opponent made the biggest mistake of his life, saying, "I didn't tap, bitch!" Tactical advantage regained, I got underhooks, based hard, got up to the cage, and devastated him with Muay Thai knees, jumping knees, and then for the finale, I landed my favorite combo just like "Big Nate," Pat Miletich, and Spencer Fischer at Miletich Fighting Systems would call it out—6-6-2-6-3, from the clinch. Uppercut, uppercut, cross, uppercut, hook. Every shot landed with laser precision. TKO!!! What a night!!! I was on fire and on the way up the ladder in the sport.

Connecting with Family

Sharing your interests with family creates a deeper bond. Whether it was discussing the latest Marvel or DC movie or debating who the strongest superhero is, these moments brought us closer. It's important to let your family into your world of interests, no matter how quirky they might seem. These shared experiences create lasting memories and strengthen the bonds of love and understanding.

Inspiring Words from Modern Heroes

Arnold Schwarzenegger, a real-life superhero in many ways, once said, "What is the point of being on this Earth if you are going to be like everyone else?" Embrace what makes you different, because that's where your true strength lies. It's about carving out your own path and living a life that is true to who you are.

Rocky Balboa once said, "Let me tell you something you already know. The world ain't all sunshine and rainbows. It's a very mean and nasty place, and I don't care how tough you are, it will beat you to your knees and keep you there permanently if you let it. You, me, or nobody is gonna hit as hard as life. But it ain't about how hard ya hit. It's about how hard you can get hit and keep moving forward. How much you can take and keep moving forward. That's how winning is done!" This powerful quote underscores the importance of resilience and determination in the face of adversity.

David Goggins, known for his relentless drive and resilience, says, "I don't stop when I'm tired. I stop when I'm done." This is the mindset of a warrior, a mindset I strive to embody every day. I, Ryan Grage, Ryan Rage, Coach Ryan, will carry the boats. I can't count how many times I've said to Landon, my oldest son, "Who's gonna carry the boats?" It's a call to action, a reminder of our strength and resilience, and the importance of stepping up to face challenges head-on.

Eminem, known for his unique style and resilience, reminds us, "I am whatever you say I am; if I wasn't, then why would you say I am." It's a powerful statement about embracing your identity and not letting others define you. Your identity is yours to shape and mold, and it should reflect your true self.

Conclusion: A Legacy of Fun and Authenticity

As I stand here, reflecting on my journey, I feel the weight of every moment that has passed and the promise of those yet to come. My dear family, friends, and all who seek inspiration, embracing your eccentric and quirky side is about celebrating what makes you unique. It's about finding joy in your passions and sharing that joy with others. This authenticity is a powerful tool for building connections and living a fulfilling life.

Life is precious and fleeting. As Iron Man said in his final moments, "Part of the journey is the end." It's a poignant reminder that every journey, every story has its culmination. But in those moments of culmination, we leave behind a legacy—a legacy of who we were, what we stood for, and the love we shared.

Remember, just as Tony Stark loved his daughter "3000," my love for you is beyond measure. It transcends time and space, an unbreakable bond. Always on your left, always loving 4,444. Let your inner superhero shine, whether it's through your interests, your personality, or your actions. This is my hope for you, my legacy, my love.

With all my heart,
Coach Ryan

Chapter 4: On Balancing Love and Discipline

Legacy of Strength and Compassion: The Power of Love and Discipline

Introduction

Hey kiddo, pull up a chair and grab a cold Corona or Ranch Water. Imagine we're sitting here, talking about life, love, and the balance you need to make it all work. Picture the spirit of Paul Walker with us, sharing stories and wisdom. This is about the most important lesson I've learned: balancing love and discipline.

The Importance of Balance

Love and discipline are the cornerstones of effective parenting and leadership. They aren't opposites but complementary forces that, when balanced, create an environment where individuals can thrive. Think of them as the wings of a bird; both are needed to soar high.

Ronald Reagan once said, "There are no constraints on the human mind, no walls around the human spirit, no barriers to our progress except those we ourselves erect." Discipline removes those self-imposed barriers, while love nurtures the spirit to push beyond boundaries. The journey is what matters. Embrace it. Whatever scares you most should be your first step.

Philosophical Insights

The great Stoic philosopher Epictetus taught us, "We have two ears and one mouth so that we can listen twice as much as we speak." This takes balance. Discipline without love can be harsh and unyielding, while love without discipline can lead to chaos and lack of direction. Together, they guide us to act wisely and compassionately.

Arnold Schwarzenegger, a man of immense discipline and love for his craft, once said, "Strength does not come from winning. Your struggles develop your strengths. When you go through hardships and decide not to surrender, that is strength." This balance of relentless discipline and passion drove him to greatness, and it can drive you too.

Practical Tips for Balancing Love and Discipline

- **Set Clear Boundaries with Compassion:** Establish rules and expectations but enforce them with understanding and empathy. When discipline is required, explain the reasons behind it, ensuring that it is perceived as guidance rather than punishment.
- **Practice Consistency:** Be consistent in your actions and decisions. Consistency in discipline builds trust and security, while consistent love fosters a sense of belonging and self-worth.
- **Encourage Independence within Limits:** Allow children to explore and make mistakes within safe boundaries. This fosters independence while ensuring they understand the importance of responsibility and the consequences of their actions.
- **Celebrate Effort and Success Equally:** Acknowledge both the effort and the outcomes. Celebrate achievements, but also recognize the hard work and perseverance that led to them.
- **Model Behavior:** Be the example you want them to follow. Show them through your actions how to balance love and discipline in their own lives.

Lessons from Great Leaders

Eric Thomas, the "Hip-Hop Preacher," speaks powerfully about overcoming adversity. He often talks about his time being homeless, saying, "I didn't know how to feel much because I was just trying to survive." His story of resilience, born from his own experiences, demonstrates how discipline turns potential into action, while love fuels the passion to keep moving forward.

David Goggins, a man who embodies the extreme balance of love and discipline, says, "You have to build calluses on your brain just like how you build calluses on your hands. Callus your mind through pain and suffering." Goggins also says the first actual rep of the workout is the one where you start to feel sore or tired. That's when the workout begins. The rest is the mental warfare and training you must endure to succeed. This applies to parenting: sometimes love means letting your children struggle and learn, fostering their resilience and strength.

A Personal Journey of Love and Discipline

When I turned 18, I was told to leave my house. I found myself living in my sister's basement, paying $150 in rent. My upbringing labeled me as disfellowshipped, a harsh blow to a young man. I worked full-time at the hospital and attended school full-time, trying to keep my head above water. The weight of being cast out and trying to find my way in the world was immense.

Despite these challenges, I realized that nursing wasn't my passion. Leaving school was tough, but it allowed me to find success in management roles in retail. This decision was pivotal, teaching me that it's okay to change course if it means finding true fulfillment.

As Coach Dad, I can be stubborn, and sometimes you might think I'm upset or mean. It's not that. I care deeply and don't want you to slip down the wrong path. The world can be unforgiving, and I stand ready to protect you with all my might. My superpowers are my love and my unwavering commitment to your well-being.

Great Grandpa Weber, my rock, always said, "If you aren't giving it your all, you haven't even started." This mantra emphasizes the importance of giving your best in everything you do. His strength and fortitude in standing for his beliefs have deeply influenced my approach to parenting and leadership.

From Powerlifting to MMA: A Journey of Resilience

My early years were marked by a deep desire to prove myself. I wasn't allowed to participate in sports due to religious restrictions. This didn't stop me from seeking physical and mental challenges later in life. I became a competitive powerlifter, channeling my frustration and ambition into strength training.

Powerlifting was just the beginning. I turned to MMA to test my limits and prove my resilience. This transition wasn't just about fighting; it was about overcoming the mental barriers that had been erected throughout my childhood. Training in Muay Thai kickboxing, jiu-jitsu, and MMA with some of the best in the field taught me discipline, focus, and the importance of pushing through pain and adversity.

Reflecting on my journey, I often think that the military would have been the best place for me. The discipline, structure, and camaraderie of military life struck a chord with my core values. I have immense respect for those who have served, and I admire the mindset and discipline they embody. Their commitment to their country and to each other is something I strive to emulate in my own life.

Conclusion: A Legacy of Balanced Strength

My dear children and grandchildren, balancing love and discipline is the key to leading a fulfilling and successful life. It's about creating an environment where you can thrive, where you feel supported and guided, and where you can grow into the best version of yourselves.

Remember the words of Marcus Aurelius, "The happiness of your life depends upon the quality of your thoughts." Fill your minds with thoughts of love and discipline, and let these principles guide you in every aspect of your life.

As you move forward, carry this legacy with you. Lead with strength, act with compassion, and always strive for balance. And remember, life is like a heavy lift: sometimes you just need to dig deep, find your grit, and always, always keep pushing.

With all my heart,

Ryan Grage (Coach Dad)

Chapter 5: On Fostering Resilience and Independence

Legacy of Selflessness: The Power of Resilience and Independence

Introduction

Friends. Today, I want to share with you the importance of resilience and independence, qualities that will guide you through life's toughest challenges. These traits are not just about personal strength but about fostering a spirit of selflessness and compassion. Let's dive into how these principles have shaped my journey and how they can guide yours.

The Importance of Resilience and Independence

Resilience is the ability to bounce back from adversity, and independence is the confidence to stand on your own. Together, they form a powerful duo that can help you navigate any storm. Remember, true strength lies not in isolation but in helping others along the way.

Taking the first step is always the hardest part. It's like ripping off a bandage—it stings at first, but once you take that leap, the path becomes clearer, and the journey gets easier. Few people muster the courage to take that initial step, but those who do set themselves apart from the rest.

Philosophical Insights

Marcus Aurelius once wrote in his Meditations, "If it is not right, do not do it; if it is not true, do not say it." This principle of integrity guides resilience and independence. When you act with integrity, you build a foundation of trust and strength within yourself. This isn't just a quote; it's a way of life that challenges us to consistently align our actions with our values. By doing so, we turn obstacles into opportunities and grow stronger in the process.

The phoenix, a symbol of resilience, rises from its ashes to live anew. This powerful imagery is tattooed on my left arm, a constant reminder of our journey. Alongside the phoenix are the initials of all our children, even Hunter and Franklin. Though they did not make it in this life, their memory inspires us to be better in every way. Just like the phoenix, our strength is not measured by the absence of adversity but by how we rise from it, transformed and determined.

The koi fish tattoo on my right arm symbolizes perseverance and the drive to overcome adversity. In Japanese culture, koi fish swimming upstream represent courage and the ability to attain high goals. Just like the koi, our family continues to swim against the current, striving to achieve greatness despite the challenges we face.

Practical Tips for Fostering Resilience and Independence

- **Encourage Risk-Taking and Learning from Mistakes:** Don't be afraid to take risks. Every failure is a lesson, and every mistake is an opportunity to learn and grow. The path to excellence is paved with repeated efforts and the courage to keep trying. Each setback is a steppingstone toward success.

- **Promote Self-Sufficiency:** Learn to stand on your own feet. Whether it's managing your finances, cooking your meals, or making decisions, self-sufficiency breeds confidence and independence. Independence is not just about surviving on your own; it's about thriving and making choices that shape your future. Developing these skills will empower you to face life's challenges head-on.

- **Build a Support Network:** Independence doesn't mean isolation. Surround yourself with people who support and uplift you. Every interaction is an opportunity to build relationships and strengthen your community. Always remember, you are being interviewed in every conversation, every connection you make. Cultivating a strong support system will provide you with the resources and encouragement needed to persevere.

- **Practice Self-Compassion:** Be kind to yourself. Acknowledge your efforts and celebrate your successes, no matter how small. Compassion for oneself is the foundation of resilience. When you treat yourself with kindness, you build the inner strength needed to face life's challenges. Self-compassion fosters a positive mindset, allowing you to navigate adversity with grace and determination.

A Personal Journey of Resilience

When I faced the darkest moments of my life, it was resilience and the support of my loved ones that pulled me through. Like Bane, forged in the shadows of darkness, I emerged stronger and more determined. My adoptive daughter may roll her eyes when I preach about being selfless, but deep down, she knows the value of these lessons.

There was a time when we lost everything during the COVID-19 pandemic. My business, our stability—it all crumbled. But from those ashes, we rebuilt our lives in Florida, finding new purpose and strength. This journey-built resilience and fostered independence. We learned that true strength lies in our ability to adapt, persevere, and support one another.

During and after the birth of our child Gunnar, we faced another significant challenge. Amber's stage 3 cancer scare had me feeling like I was taking constant body shots from my old sparing partners. The uncertainty and fear were overwhelming, but we leaned on our resilience and the support of our family and friends. Fully recovered, this experience only strengthened our resolve to cherish each moment and support each other through life's hurdles.

The Power of Family and Community

Our family, including those we have welcomed into our tribe, has shown that together, we can accomplish anything. The koi fish tattoo swimming upstream on my arm symbolizes this relentless drive and determination. We got this! As a family, we support and uplift each other, facing every challenge head-on and never giving up.

Building strong relationships is crucial. Always build your relationships and remember that every interaction is an opportunity to leave a positive impression. Every chat, every conversation, and every connection you make, they all matter. By nurturing our connections and fostering a sense of community, we create a support system that enhances our resilience and independence.

Lessons from My Life

Reflecting on my own journey, there were countless times when the odds seemed insurmountable. Whether it was overcoming personal tragedies, rebuilding after financial losses, or simply finding the strength to move forward each day, resilience was my guiding light. Independence gave me the confidence to make tough decisions and stand by them.

Resilience taught me to view challenges not as roadblocks, but as opportunities for growth. Independence allowed me to take control of my destiny, shaping my path with determination and self-reliance. These qualities were not just cultivated in isolation, but through the love, support, and strength of those around me.

Inspiring the Next Generation

To all of you, my children, grandchildren, friends, and loved ones, I want you to know that fostering resilience and independence is not just about personal strength; it's about being selfless, compassionate, and always ready to help others. These traits will guide you through life's toughest challenges and help you find purpose and fulfillment.

The happiness of your life depends on the quality of your thoughts. Fill your minds with thoughts of resilience, independence, and selflessness. Let these principles guide you in every aspect of your life. Embrace challenges as opportunities to grow and rely on your inner strength to overcome adversity.

As you move forward, carry this legacy with you. Be strong, be compassionate, and always strive to help others. This is my hope for you, my legacy, my love.

With all my heart,

Coach Ryan

Chapter 6: On Nurturing Emotional Intelligence Legacy of Emotional Strength: The Power of Emotional Intelligence

Introduction

Gather around, everyone. Today, we're diving into the essence of what makes us truly strong—emotional intelligence. This chapter is about understanding our feelings, harnessing them, and using them to forge stronger bonds and a life full of purpose. Think of this as my version of a CrossFit WOD, like Murph or Clovis (tough, relentless, and transformative). These workouts, full of running and bodyweight challenges, pushed me to my limits. They taught me to embrace what I wasn't good at, to find strength in struggle. Just like those workouts, nurturing emotional intelligence is about facing the toughest parts of ourselves and emerging stronger.

The Power of Emotional Intelligence

Emotional intelligence is more than just a buzzword. It's the key to navigating life's storms with grace and resilience. It's the ability to recognize our emotions, understand them, and use that insight to connect with others on a deeper level. It's about being in tune with our inner world and letting that guide our interactions with the world around us.

Embrace the Struggle

Challenges have always been the greatest teachers. Just like the grueling workouts that tested my limits, emotional intelligence requires us to face our vulnerabilities head-on. It's about feeling the burn of discomfort and pushing through it, knowing that on the other side lies growth and strength.

When I think back to those times when life seemed overwhelming, I realized that true strength wasn't just about physical prowess or sheer will. It was about understanding my emotions, letting them inform my actions, and using them to build bridges with those around me. It was about learning to listen—not just with my ears but with my heart.

Building Emotional Strength

In our home, we always had a place where feelings were welcome. Amber set the tone that no creativity was unacceptable, allowing our children to grow by leaps and bounds. Our slime station in the basement was a place where they could express themselves freely and get messy. Be creative without fear of judgment. It's essential to cultivate an environment where everyone feels safe to express themselves without judgment. This space is where real connection happens, where we understand each other's fears, joys, and struggles.

Active Listening is Key

One of the most powerful tools in emotional intelligence is active listening. It's about being fully present, letting the other person speak without interrupting, and really hearing what they're saying. It's about acknowledging their emotions and responding with empathy and understanding. This is an area I continually work on; it can be my biggest strength when I follow my own advice.

Empathy: The Glue That Binds Us

Empathy is the heart of emotional intelligence. It's the ability to step into someone else's shoes, to understand their feelings, and to respond with compassion. It's not about fixing their problems but about standing with them, sharing their pain, and celebrating their victories. Remember, empathy and sympathy are not the same—never be fooled by the wolf in sheep's clothing.

Mastering Emotional Regulation

Managing our emotions is crucial. It's about finding healthy ways to express anger, sadness, or frustration. Techniques like deep breathing, meditation, or simply taking a moment to reflect can help us maintain our emotional balance. Don't be scared to blow off steam by walking around the block; this can release the endorphins needed to make the best-informed decision. Your mind will rush to act—don't.

My Journey with Emotional Intelligence

In my life, emotional intelligence has been my anchor. There were times when the weight of the world seemed too heavy to bear. But it was through understanding my emotions and those of others that I found my way.

I faced many battles, both physical and emotional. From CrossFit competitions to personal struggles. I learned to embrace the pain, to see it as a path to growth. Just like those challenging workouts, emotional intelligence requires us to push past our limits, to embrace the discomfort, and to come out stronger on the other side.

Lessons from the Trenches

In those moments of darkness, I found that the greatest strength comes from compassion and understanding. It's about being there for each other, lifting each other up, and finding strength in our shared humanity. Whether it was comforting a friend in need or facing my own demons, I learned that true strength is measured not by how much we can endure alone, but by how much we can give and receive love and support.

When I look at my family, my heart swells with pride. Each one of you has faced your battles, and I've seen you grow stronger with every challenge. Whether it was the resilience shown in the face of personal loss or the unwavering support during tough times, you've embodied the essence of emotional intelligence. You've taught me that the heart of strength lies in our connections, in our ability to empathize, to understand, and to support each other.

Inspiration from the Journey

"The most important conversations you'll ever have are the ones you'll have with yourself." This rings true in every aspect of life. Those conversations, the ones where we confront our fears and doubts, are the ones that shape our character and our destiny. They are the foundation of emotional strength.

Live fully, love deeply, and cherish every moment. This legacy reminds us that emotional intelligence is about being present, appreciating the people around us, and making every connection count.

Embrace the grind. Want success as badly as you want to breathe. That applies to emotional intelligence too. It's about wanting to understand ourselves and others so deeply that it becomes our driving force. It's about waking up every day with a hunger to connect, to empathize, and to grow.

True strength lies in our response to life's challenges. We have power over our mind, not external events. It's about mastering our emotions, staying calm in the face of adversity, and using every experience as a lesson.

When the world seemed to be against us, it was our ability to connect, to understand, and to support each other that pulled us through. From the darkest days to the brightest moments, emotional intelligence has been our guiding star. It's what has kept us grounded, what has driven us to keep going, no matter the odds.

Community and Compassion

Being emotionally intelligent is not limited to personal interactions; it's about extending that empathy and support to our community. When power outages hit during natural disasters, our gym became a refuge for those in need. We opened our doors to anyone affected, offering warmth and safety. We would personally take food to families who were struggling, ensuring they had enough to eat. No one left our gym hungry; there was always a plate of food ready, even if they showed up with a family of four or six.

These acts of kindness and support were not just about providing physical comfort but about showing empathy and compassion. They were about understanding the struggles of others and stepping up to help in whatever way we could. This is emotional intelligence in action—using our awareness of others' emotions to make a positive impact.

Conclusion: The Legacy of Emotional Intelligence

As you walk this path of life, remember that emotional intelligence is not just a skill; it's a way of life. It's about understanding yourself and others, about building connections that are deep and meaningful. It's about-facing life's challenges with courage and compassion, knowing that every struggle is a step towards greater strength.

Carry this legacy with you. Let your hearts be your guide, your compassion your strength, and your love your driving force. Be there for each other, support each other, and never forget that the true measure of our strength is in how well we connect with and uplift those around us.

With all my heart,

Coach Ryan

Chapter 7: On the Power of Presence

Legacy of Strength: The Journey of Resilience and Rebirth

Introduction

My dear children and grandchildren, life is a series of battles, and each of us has our own to fight. Today, I want to share a deeply personal journey—my rise as a local MMA star, my transition to CrossFit, the tragedy and loss that scarred me, and the rebirth that followed. This chapter is about the power of presence, resilience, and finding purpose through unimaginable challenges.

Rising as a Local MMA Star

My journey began in the brutal and exhilarating world of Mixed Martial Arts (MMA) at the legendary Miletich Fighting Systems gym in Bettendorf, Iowa. The renowned Pat Miletich welcomed me onto his team with zero experience because of my strength from years of powerlifting. Training side by side with top fighters, who are now UFC legends, I was immersed in an environment of fierce competitors who treated this as their full-time job.

There was only one fight I lost in my entire MMA career. It was a moment I quit on myself before my body was done. It was for the Illinois Amateur Championship belt. I fought at 185 pounds, and it was a struggle every time for me to make weight. I showed up, and the 185-pound guy backed out. The promoter said he was "unable to fight." I had just barely made weight, and now he comes to me and wants me to fight a light heavyweight at 205 pounds. I feared nothing, so without hesitation, I said yes. I was still in the zone, still ready. I had no fear. I would destroy these 205 guys just like any other.

One hour from the fights, the 205 guy pulls out as well. The promoter says I can still fight if I fight for the heavyweight amateur belt. I am going to tell you the truth, I got scared. I still said yes, but I let a little doubt in. This guy had cut zero weight and had been adding calories the whole night while I starved myself for the last week. He weighed in at 225 pounds. I gave him a 40-pound advantage. He was a college linebacker and still had the build. We were in a small town, not my own. It was his crowd. There were serious racial concerns ongoing for our team because we had Black and Mexican fighters on our team. There were so many tangents ongoing in my brain.

It was here that I learned many lessons. No music to walk out to—they didn't have speakers that played for out-of-town fighters, just the hometown guy. I like my walkout music. "Till I Collapse" by Eminem... when that beat drops, damn.

We get in the cage, the fight starts, and we bump fists. I decide ground and pound is my goal. Though I now know if I would have just trusted my Muay Thai, I would have destroyed this guy. We end up on the ground after I surprised him with some shots against the cage. I now know he is scared big time. I can win this fight. We go to the ground, and I know once I rise off his chest, this fight is 20-30 seconds from being over. I will ruthlessly ground and pound him, and the referee will step in when he is unconscious. I had that in me. I was that fierce competitor.

We go to the ground, and his giant ass bicep and pec have me in a guillotine choke. Whatever, I get out of these for breakfast. Well, we were not that sweaty yet because I rushed everything. I rushed the takedown and rushed going to the ground. I got caught. I used every tactic I could to escape, but it was no use. And I tapped. What the what, Ryan? You don't tap! Who was this person? I got up and congratulated him on his win. He won. He beat me. He made me who I never wanted to be again. I let external conflicts cloud my mind and judgment. I let it be okay for him to take the belt. I still remember his name and still have the video saved. Anytime I need a reminder, I watch that fight. I feared what would happen to others that I loved if I had won that fight. We might not have made it out of town. What a night. Spencer "The King" Fisher was a great coach that night. He had us protected in many ways. I am forever thankful for his coaching skills.

MMA taught me the value of presence. In the ring, you must be fully present, fully aware. Every moment counts, every decision can be the difference between victory and defeat. This intense focus and presence became a cornerstone of my life, both in and out of the ring.

Transitioning to CrossFit

After years of MMA, I sought a new challenge—one that would push me physically without the constant risk of injury. We initially started CrossFit as an assistance to our cardio sessions for MMA. Our coach, "Big Nate," made us do pull-ups, push-ups, and air squats after two hours of gi and no-gi Jiu Jitsu, followed by two hours of kickboxing technique and sparring. CrossFit quickly became my new arena. The workouts were grueling, demanding a different kind of strength and endurance. It was a competition against myself, a daily battle to be better than I was the day before.

CrossFit brought back the camaraderie I loved in MMA, but it also offered a community. Together, we faced the toughest workouts, cheered each other on, and celebrated every victory, no matter how small. It was here that I learned the power of presence—being there for others, supporting them, and finding joy in their successes.

The Accident and Rehabilitation

In 2011, my life took a drastic turn. I was involved in an industrial accident at a corn processing plant. A small explosion left me with skin hanging from my arms, face, and leg. The pain was excruciating, not just physically but emotionally. I stripped and got in the shower station, thinking I could get help by using my radio, but I couldn't because it had been left inoperable by the explosion. I made my way down the stairs to the main floor of the processing plant and found another shower. This is where a worker found me and was able to alert the emergency squad. From there, I was addressed by the on-site nurse, and then quickly the local ambulance took me to the hospital. The emergency room knew that they didn't want me anywhere near their hospital and called for the helicopter. I was life-flighted to Iowa City.

I remember getting to the hospital and the doors of the ambulance opened. My dad was there. They had asked me on the way to the hospital if there was anyone that I could think to call that would be at the hospital for me. I don't know how I remembered. I knew I needed my dad. I was in the emergency room for less than an hour. I was stabilized, and my flight headed to Iowa City where I had extensive surgery within an hour and a half to two hours from being burnt. I was fortunate to have the University of Iowa by us and so close. I was treated by the best doctors and with no skin grafts and very minimal scarring to this day externally, I am very lucky to be alive. If I would have ingested the liquid that had exploded by gasping as you typically would during a scary situation, I would have died. My lungs would have been destroyed. It was 235 to 250-degree liquid ethanol.

The road to recovery was long and arduous. Fitness, which had always been my strength, became my rehabilitation. I used fitness to rebuild my body and my spirit. Each workout was a step towards healing, each lift a symbol to my resilience. I embraced the pain and the struggle, knowing that every drop of sweat, every ounce of effort was bringing me closer to recovery. The accident had scarred me, but it also forged a new strength within me.

The rehab was tough, and I was told many things that I would not be able to do. I decided that those were not going to be things for me that I could not do. I refused to listen to the doctors when they said I probably shouldn't fight, and I made it my goal and my drive and passion to find a way to fight again.

The Intense Training Regimen

Training to fight again was going to take more than anything I had ever had in me for training. I was lucky enough to train with the former heavyweight champion of the world at the time, and train alongside 20 to

30 of the best fighters in the Midwest. The training regimen for that fight was the most intense I had ever undergone. It was like Rocky IV, where he trains alone in Russia with no machines, just using what was available to him. The night of the fight came, and I was emotionally detached. Nothing changed in me as I warmed up. As I was in the back, I saw him. It didn't bother me. I knew what was about to occur. I had trained for every possible scenario. In his intro video, he was a little arrogant, and it really bothered me, because I knew he had no chance at beating me.

We walked out of the back with my entourage from the gym. "Till I Collapse" was playing by Eminem. The smoke, the fog, everything was going, and I was ready. And yet nothing changed. We entered the ring. The bell went. We hit gloves, and the fight began. I stood for a quick moment, and I quickly used every possible opportunity I could to punch my way in and gain a good lock on him. From there, I used many jujitsu techniques, standing up and on the ground, to suck the life out of my opponent. We stood up, and I'm not going to lie, he hit me once. It was the last time I was going to get hit. I landed an uppercut, nearly missed, and left hook, which I thought was going to be the end. But my left hook really just glazed off his head. I hit him more with my forearm.

It took him to the ground, and he wasn't unconscious at the moment. So I went and followed him to the ground with hammer fists. After maybe one or two too many punches, the referee came in. He was completely knocked out. I raised my hand. I was excited. Yet, nothing changed again. At this moment, I knew I had to be done with fighting. I didn't want it anymore like I thought I did. And I was ready to move on and do something different with my life.

Marrying Amber Nichole Grage

In 2012, I married the love of my life, Amber Nichole Grage. Our journey together was one of unwavering support and shared dreams. From the moment we said, "I do," we had a goal to share a child with our combined DNA. Amber's strength and resilience have always been a source of inspiration for me. Her love and dedication have been the bedrock of our family, and together, we have faced life's greatest challenges and celebrated its most profound joys.

The Tragic Loss of 2013

In 2013, our family faced an unimaginable tragedy. We lost two children, Hunter Clyde and Franklin Cash, due to premature birth. The pain of losing a child is indescribable. It shatters you, leaving a void that can never be filled. Yet, in the depths of this sorrow, I found a new resolve.

Hunter Clyde Grage came into the world on March 26, 2013. He was so small and so fragile, born prematurely in Iowa City after a high-risk pregnancy. He just wasn't strong enough to survive and lived just about an hour. We were able to hold him and show him love. He never did wrong in this world. I think he is many parts of our youngest son, Gunnar.

The saddest part was driving away from the hospital without your son. Your DNA. You had to leave him there. As a dad, not being able to watch over your legacy is chilling to the soul.

We quickly decided to try again. On November 3, 2013, tragedy struck again. Amber was at work, and I was watching the kids. Her coworkers called and said she was in labor and heading to the hospital. When I arrived, the same situation was occurring. Just over 21 weeks, and Franklin Cash Grage was on his way.

It was here where I was pushed hardest. Amber had to have additional surgeries to stop the bleeding. I had to manage the newborn that wouldn't make it and my wife's health. I had to have the heart of a warrior and fighter. There were no options. This is where I learned the truest test. As the quote goes, "Nobody cares about your problems. If you've got problems, own them. You are the only one that will get you out."

Rising from the Ashes: The Birth of CrossFit Port Byron

In 2014, from the ashes of tragedy and loss, we founded CrossFit Port Byron (CFPB). This gym was more than just a place to work out; it was a community, a sanctuary, a place where people came together to push their limits and support each other. CFPB became legendary, impacting countless lives and creating lifelong bonds.

At CFPB, we faced the toughest workouts, celebrated the biggest victories, and supported each other through the hardest times. The gym embodied the spirit of resilience and the power of presence. It was proof to what we could achieve when we came together as a community.

Specific Stories of Resilience and Community

The Murph Workout: Every Memorial Day, we honored fallen soldiers with the Murph workout. It was a grueling test of endurance and strength, but it was also a time of unity. We pushed through the pain together, supporting each other every step of the way. The sense of accomplishment at the end was indescribable—a testament to our collective resilience.

Choose a Hero WOD Day: This became a huge part of our community's 4th of July celebration. We selected various hero workouts, each representing a fallen hero, and completed them together. It was a powerful reminder of sacrifice and strength.

Clovis Training: Once every year, we trained for Clovis, a workout consisting of a 10-mile run and 150 burpee pull-ups. The preparation and completion of this workout were tests of mental and physical endurance that brought us closer as a community.

The Squat Cycles: Oh, the squat cycles! These were periods of intense squatting routines that built not just physical strength but also mental toughness. They were grueling but incredibly rewarding.

Technique Thursday: Dedicated to perfecting our forms and techniques, these sessions ensured that we were always improving and pushing our limits safely and effectively.

Partner Saturday: These days were special. We paired up for challenging workouts, supporting and motivating each other. It was a time to bond, to cheer each other on, and to strengthen our community ties.

Conclusion: A Legacy of Presence and Resilience

My dear children and grandchildren, my journey has been one of battles fought and lessons learned. From rising as an MMA star to founding a legendary CrossFit gym, each step has taught me the importance of presence and resilience. It's about being there for each other, embracing challenges, and finding strength in community.

Remember, life will test you in ways you cannot imagine. But it's in those moments of struggle that you will find your true strength. Be present, be resilient, and support each other. This is my legacy, my hope, my love for you.

With all my heart, Ryan Grage (Coach Ryan)

Chapter 8: Moments Captured - The Essence of a Life Well Lived

Legacy of Strength: Embracing Every Moment

Introduction

My dear children, grandchildren, and everyone seeking motivation, life is a series of moments woven together with threads of joy, pain, triumph, and despair. As I look back on our journey, the photographs we have taken are not just pictures but fragments of our soul, capturing the essence of our experiences and the depth of our emotions. This chapter is dedicated to the snapshots of our lives, the moments that have shaped us, and the legacy we continue to build together.

Lead by Example

"Lead by example, they are watching." This mantra has been at the core of my philosophy. Seeing the pictures of you, my children, lifting weights, running, and participating in CrossFit fills my heart with pride. These images are not just about physical fitness but about instilling values of hard work, perseverance, and dedication from a young age. Each photo is a testament to the importance of setting a positive example, knowing that you are always observing and learning from me.

I remember the day you, Landon, my eldest, decided to take on the challenge of lifting a weight that seemed impossible. The determination in your eyes, the strain on your face, and the moment of triumph when you succeeded are forever etched in my memory. Sometimes, all you needed was a little nudge from Dad to believe in your talent. When you showed what you were truly capable of, man, I couldn't be prouder. It was a powerful reminder that our children are capable of extraordinary feats when they see their parents leading by example. Your heart, the heart of a gladiator, always showed through, and watching you realize your potential has been one of the greatest joys of my life.

The Power of Community

The images of our CrossFit community are a vivid reminder of the strength and support we found in each other. From group workouts to celebrations, every picture tells the story of a family bound by shared goals and mutual respect. We lifted each other up, both literally and figuratively. These moments encapsulate the power of community and the bonds that transcend the gym walls.

I think back to the day after as a massive tornado leveled the neighboring community. The sense of camaraderie was palpable as everyone came together, rolling up their sleeves and working tirelessly to help those affected. Our gym became a sanctuary, offering showers and restrooms to those in need. The photos from that day capture not just the physical labor but the emotional strength and unity that defined us as a community. Our doors were always open when the community needed us, and those moments of solidarity are forever etched in my heart.

Celebrations and Achievements

The photographs of competitions, medals, and victories are not just about winning but about the journey. "I may not be the fittest, I may not be the strongest, but I'll be damned if I'm not trying my hardest." This spirit of relentless effort and determination is captured in each image of us pushing our limits and striving for excellence. These moments of triumph are a testament to our hard work and the resilience that defines us.

Standing on the podium at the 2019 Master's World of Weightlifting Championship, taking third place, was an experience that sent chills through my entire body. The USA swept first to third place, and as the National Anthem played, I felt a surge of pride and honor. I was representing THE USA! I went 6 for 6, snatching 125 and clean and jerking 156. My opponent, who was vying for my medal, failed a weight that was too heavy because I had pulled him into the deep end. I had the best back-room coach, Amber, my amazing wife, who had placed in the top 10 the day before. It was electric. Each photo from that day reminds me of the power of perseverance and the joy of achieving something greater than myself.

Family and Love

"All because two people fell in love." The family portraits, candid shots, and moments of togetherness highlight the foundation of everything we do—love and family. These images are a constant reminder of the love that Amber Nichole Grage and I share, a love that has created and nurtured a beautiful family. From beach outings to family gatherings, these moments capture the essence of our love and the joy of being together.

One of my favorite photographs is of us at the beach, with the sun setting in the background. We were all there, laughing, playing, and simply enjoying each other's company. It's a picture that captures the pure, unfiltered joy of being surrounded by loved ones. These are the moments that define our lives and remind us of what truly matters.

Embracing Challenges

The pictures of intense workouts, exhausted but satisfied faces, and moments of pure determination embody our commitment to embracing challenges. "When I lost all of my excuses, I found my results." The first rep is when your mind lets you wander and feel like it's getting hard. The workout is just now beginning. These images are a testament to the sweat, effort, and perseverance that have been pivotal in our journey. They remind us that through hard work and resilience, we can overcome any obstacle.

Training with CrossFit Kilo 2 in Iowa City, where they lived and died by the quote, "Get the job, Do the job!" was a transformative experience. There is a particular photo of me totally collapsed at the Iowa City competition where we went up against some top athletes in the US Midwest. It captures the raw emotion of pushing beyond my limits, of giving everything I had. It is a reminder that true strength is found not in avoiding challenges but in facing them head-on, no matter how insurmountable they may seem.

Community and Support

Images of our community events, pool parties, and gatherings reflect the joy and camaraderie that have been a cornerstone of our lives. These moments of laughter, fun, and shared experiences are what make life rich and fulfilling. They remind us that while individual achievements are important, it is the connections we build with others that truly matter.

One of the most memorable experiences was hosting a pool party at our home. The laughter of children, the clinking of glasses, and the shared stories of triumph and hardship created an atmosphere of pure joy. The photos from that day capture the essence of community, of being there for each other, and of celebrating life's simple pleasures. The food, the people, the activities like playing volleyball, kickball, and softball—everything contributed to the magic of that day.

The Next Generation

Photographs of the younger members of our community lifting weights, participating in workouts, and enjoying the environment are a promise of the future. "Don't be afraid to lift heavy; you are stronger than you think." Building the future by building a legacy, they are always watching. These images are a celebration of the next generation, who are growing up with the values of strength, resilience, and community that we hold dear.

Personal Experiences: Finding Strength in Community

One email came in late at night from Alex Bitler, a man who was on the verge of making a life-changing decision. He wrote about his struggles with motivation, smoking, drinking, and filling his void with drugs. He expressed his desire for a better way and the pain he was in, both physically and emotionally. I followed up with him at midnight to make sure he was okay and ready to work out in the morning. This act of reaching out changed his life. He found a community that supported him, and he transformed his life through fitness and the bonds we formed. Alex is now a motivational speaker, a beacon of hope demonstrating how our community has the power to save lives.

MaKenna's Moment of Triumph

One of my most cherished memories is of my third child, MaKenna, winning a pull-up competition during a break at a CrossFit event. She held onto the bar for the entire minute, her determination visible to everyone in attendance. Against a seasoned CrossFit athlete who had competed at regionals, MaKenna performed over 20 kipping pull-ups. The crowd watched in awe as she showcased incredible strength and tenacity. This moment is a powerful reminder of the values we instill in our children and the extraordinary potential within them.

London's Dance and Cheer Journey

Watching my second child, London, compete in dance and cheer throughout her life has been a source of immense pride and joy. The grit and dedication it takes to excel in dance for all those years are nothing short of inspiring. London's love for fitness manifests in a different style than mine, and it fills my heart with happiness to see her passion.

One of the most memorable experiences was participating in the Daddy-Daughter dances. These moments, when I joined a group of about ten other dads willing to embarrass ourselves, were some of the best times of my life. The pure joy on London's face as we danced together is a memory I will always cherish. It wasn't just about the dance; it was about the connection and the happiness we shared. Those photos of us on stage, with our daughters beaming beside us, are treasured snapshots of our bond and the love that drives everything we do.

Gunnar's First Experience with a Rower

One of the most unforgettable moments was Gunnar's first experience with a rower. He had just started walking, and we were coaching a class of twenty people. Gunnar walked right over to a rower, moved the seat on the rollers, and fell right onto the rower rail, splitting his eyebrow open. He needed stitches, and while Amber and our dearest friend took him to the ER, I finished coaching the class. This incident was a poignant lesson in life and resilience. It reminded us that even in moments of crisis, we have the strength to continue and support each other through every challenge. Gunnar is always looking for the thrill of the rush, fearlessly skateboarding, scooter riding, and taking on any other daring activity.

Conclusion

My dear children, grandchildren, and everyone seeking motivation, these photographs are more than just images; they are a chronicle of our journey, capturing the highs and lows, the joy and pain, and the essence of our lives. They remind us of where we have been, what we have achieved, and the legacy we are building together. As you look through these pictures, may you find inspiration, strength, and a deep sense of connection to our family and community.

These moments, captured forever in these images, are the threads that weave the tapestry of our lives. They are a tribute to the love, resilience, and strength that define us. May these memories serve as a source of strength and inspiration for generations to come. Every snapshot tells a story, every smile and tear a chapter in our ongoing saga. Cherish these moments, for they are the essence of a life well lived.

With all my love and dedication,

Ryan, Coach Ryan, and Coach Dad

Chapter 9: The Dark Side of Ryan Rage

Introduction

In the life of every warrior, there comes a time when the battles fought are not against external enemies but against the shadows within. For me, Ryan Grage, a long-time business owner and father of four, this battle came when I lost half of my members to a new gym started by my former head coach. This chapter delves into the darkest period of my life, a time when the light of Marcus Aurelius seemed distant, and I felt more like Peter Quill in Infinity War—letting personal feelings overshadow what was better for the common good of everyone.

The Betrayal

The pain of betrayal is a deep wound that leaves lasting scars. The head coach, once a trusted ally and integral part of CrossFit Port Byron (CFPB), had become a rival. I ended her opportunity to coach at CFPB far too late, underestimating the power struggle that was brewing. The memories and bonds we had shared were overshadowed by her ambition and hunger for control.

Jealousy and the desire for dominance took root in her actions. She began to manipulate and gaslight the members, slowly eroding the trust and unity we had built. The whispers and doubts spread like wildfire, turning the gym—a place once filled with fellowship and mutual respect—into a battleground of conflicting loyalties.

I recall the days leading up to the mass exodus of my members. The gym, once a sanctuary of sweat and camaraderie, became a hostile environment where division and suspicion reigned. The betrayal was not just a professional setback; it was a personal attack that left me rocked, like a right cross to the face.

The Impact

I was not the shining star of Marcus Aurelius during these dark days. I felt like a fallen warrior, aimlessly wandering through the battlefield of my life. The power struggle had drained me, and the once vibrant community I had built with my sweat and tears was fracturing. The loss of members wasn't just a blow to my business; it was a loss of what I had achieved with each member.

The resolve that had fueled my journey seemed extinguished, replaced by a deep-seated despair. My best friend, a foundational member of CFPB, was among those who left. Our friendship, once a source of strength and joy, became strained and distant. The Facebook posts, filled with accusations and hurt, only deepened the wound.

The Emotional Toll

The emotional toll of the gym split was immense. I had always been a pillar of strength, not just for my family but for my community. The members who left were not just clients; they were friends, confidants, and companions in the journey of fitness and life. The severing of these ties felt like an amputation, a part of my soul ripped away.

Maintaining each member took significant emotional deposits daily, weekly, and monthly. The energy it consumed was immense, from motivating and coaching to celebrating their victories and supporting them through their struggles. Each interaction was an investment of my spirit and losing them felt like watching those investments crumble.

The Struggle to Rebuild

In the aftermath of the exodus, I struggled to rebuild both my business and my spirit. The gym, now half-empty, echoed with memories of better days. Each empty spot where a member once stood was a stark reminder of the loss. Disloyalty had not just taken people; it had taken a part of my identity.

I fought to regain my footing, to find a way back to the warrior I once was. The teachings of Marcus Aurelius, Seneca, and Epictetus, which had once been my guiding light, seemed dimmed.

Epictetus, who was once a slave and later became a great philosopher, offers profound wisdom for such dark times. He said, "We suffer not from the events in our lives, but from our judgment about them." I began to see that my suffering was rooted not in the betrayal itself, but in how I perceived and reacted to it. Epictetus also taught, "No man is free who is not master of himself." This reminded me that to rebuild, I first had to master my own emotions and mindset.

Finding Strength in Darkness

It was during this time of darkness that I began to understand the true nature of resilience. Seneca once said, "Difficulties strengthen the mind, as labor does the body." I realized that this loss was not the end, but a new beginning. The pain I felt was forging a stronger, more resilient spirit within me.

I found inspiration from motivational speaker Eric Thomas, who famously said, "Don't cry to quit, cry to keep going." This chant became a lifeline for me, reminding me that tears were not a sign of weakness but a validation of my relentless drive. Eric Thomas' words fueled my resolve, encouraging me to push through the pain and continue my path.

Captain America once said, "I can do this all day." This quote from the Marvel universe struck a chord with me. I realized that my battle was not just physical but mental and emotional as well. The grind didn't stop just because things got tough; in fact, it intensified. I embraced the sleepless nights, the relentless hustle, knowing that every moment spent fighting was a step towards reclaiming my strength and rebuilding my life.

I began to rebuild, not just my gym, but my spirit. I found solace in the small victories, the new members who joined, and the loyal ones who stayed. Slowly, the gym started to come alive again, a phoenix rising from the ashes of betrayal.

Conclusion

To all who seek inspiration, this chapter of my life was a test of my spirit and resilience. The betrayal and loss I faced were profound, shaking me to my core. But it was through this darkness that I found a deeper understanding of strength and perseverance. The power struggles, the manipulations, and the loss of friends taught me valuable lessons about trust, loyalty, and the true essence of community.

As you face your own battles in life, remember that even in the darkest times, there is a way forward. The shadows may obscure your path, but they can never extinguish the light within. Find strength in your struggles and know that every impediment you face is an opportunity for growth and transformation.

Grages always move forward; we always look for the next opportunity to succeed. Never allow yourself to be a deer in the headlights. Always have a plan for the next step in the right direction.

With all my heart,

Ryan Charles Grage

Chapter 10: The Continuation of Struggle

Introduction

Life is a relentless series of trials, and just when you think you've weathered the worst storm, another wave comes crashing down. For me, the struggle continued even after beginning to stem the bleeding from the gym split that nearly broke me. Just as I was finding my footing again, the world was hit by an unprecedented crisis—COVID-19. Then came the darkest days of our journey.

Inevitable Gym Closure Email

Dear Members, (on March, 2020)

I hope this message finds you and your loved ones safe and healthy. As the COVID-19 situation continues to unfold, it is with a heavy heart that I must inform you that we have been ordered to close the gym temporarily.

We understand the importance of maintaining your fitness routine, especially during these challenging times. To support you, we are posting home workouts for you to follow and providing online nutrition coaching and goal-setting sessions. Our commitment to your health and wellness remains as strong as ever.

We are also creating small equipment packages that can be picked up at the gym for home use. We will write daily workouts that align with the equipment being lent out. These packages will need to be returned within a reasonable amount of time so that others can benefit from them as well. Please ensure that all equipment is cleaned appropriately before returning it.

We are doing everything we can to adapt and continue our mission of providing health and wellness to our community. However, we need your support now more than ever. Your continued membership and engagement are crucial to helping us navigate through this difficult period.

We will keep you updated with any new developments and the eventual reopening of the gym. In the meantime, please do not hesitate to reach out with any questions or concerns. Thank you again for your unwavering support. Together, we will get through this.

Stay strong and healthy,

Ryan Grage
Owner, CFPB

The Global Shutdown

When COVID-19 struck, the world came to a standstill. Gyms, like many other businesses, were forced to shut their doors. The vibrant energy of CrossFit Port Byron (CFPB) was replaced by an eerie silence. But even in the face of this global shutdown, we believed in the strength of our community and its ability to persevere. We allowed members to take equipment home so they could work out in their garages, basements, kitchens, or wherever they could find space. However, the members quickly faded; they needed the four walls of the gym to work out in.

During this time, we even expanded, becoming part owners of another location. It was a bold move, but an unwavering belief in the fitness community. But as the pandemic dragged on and the second shutdown hit, the steam was taken out of our engines. We were no longer able to pay the gym bills without assistance from outside full-time careers. Both Amber and I worked full-time jobs while running two gyms, desperately trying to keep the engine turning and reignite the fitness flame in the community.

A Decade in Fitness

For nearly a decade, I had been fully immersed in the fitness industry. From the moment I rose from the ashes of being burnt at ADM, I had poured my heart and soul into building CFPB. Like a koi fish swimming against the current, I had navigated the challenges and come out stronger. But now, the game was over. There was nothing left in me to give to the community.

The financial burden was immense. The emotional toll was even greater. I had dedicated my life to fitness, to helping others find their strength and resilience. Now, I found myself struggling to keep my own head above water. The sense of defeat was overwhelming, and the future seemed bleak.

A New Brotherhood

Amidst this turmoil, I met someone who would become a brother to me— Alex Bitler, who I mentioned in the previous chapter. Our paths crossed at a time when I was rough around the edges, battle-hardened by years of struggle. This was the period when our brotherhood was forged. In Alex, I found a kindred spirit, someone who understood the depth of my struggles and stood by me through it all. Alex Bitler defines what a real brother should be—loyal, understanding, and unwavering in support.

We bonded over our shared love for fitness and our relentless pursuit of personal growth. Alex saw the raw, unfiltered version of me—the man who had studied philosophy for the better part of a decade and who, despite the hardships, was mentally on top of his coaching game. Together, we navigated the final years of my run in the fitness industry, finding strength in our brotherhood.

The Philosophy of Resilience

Throughout these years, the teachings of philosophers had been my guiding light. Their words of wisdom had helped me stay grounded and focused. Even in the darkest times, their teachings reminded me that true strength lies in how we respond to adversity.

Epictetus once said, "It's not what happens to you, but how you react to it that matters." This philosophy became my creed. The obstacles I faced, from the deception of a trusted friend to the global pandemic, were not just setbacks but opportunities for growth and transformation.

Donald Trump once said, "What separates the winners from the losers is how a person reacts to each new twist of fate." These words struck a chord with me. The challenges I faced were not the end, but the beginning of a new chapter. I realized that my reaction to adversity would define my journey.

The Final Chapter

As the pandemic continued, it became clear that my time in the fitness industry was coming to an end. The financial and emotional strain was too great, and I had to make the difficult decision to step away. It was a heartbreaking realization, but one that was necessary for my own well-being and the future of my family.

I remember the day I closed the doors of CFPB for the last time. The gym that had been my sanctuary, my passion, and my life's work was now a memory. But even in that moment of profound loss, I found a sense of peace. I had given everything I had to my community, and it was time to move forward.

Conclusion

To anyone who needs inspiration, this chapter of my life was one of powerful struggle and loss. But it was also a view into the resilience of the human spirit. The challenges I faced during this time were immense, but they also shaped me into the man I am today.

As you navigate your own journeys, remember that life is filled with obstacles. It is how we respond to these challenges that defines us. Find strength in adversity, and always seek the lessons that each struggle has to offer. Know that even in the darkest times, there is a way forward.

With all my heart,
Ryan Grage - Owner & Operator
Grage Enterprises LLC

Chapter 11: The Road to Closure and Regrowth

Introduction

There comes a time in every warrior's journey when the battles fought and the scars earned call for a retreat, not in defeat, but in search of renewal. After years of struggle, betrayal, and the crushing weight of the pandemic, it became clear that the path to healing and growth lay not in staying but in moving forward. This chapter is about our decision to move to Florida, near the beautiful beaches, and the new beginnings that awaited us there.

A Fresh Start

The constant reminders of the struggles we had endured and the whisperings of a world that had turned harsh had become too much to bear. The memories of the gym split, the financial strain and the emotional toll of the past years were deeply embedded in the walls of CrossFit Port Byron. The town of Port Byron and the Midwest held memories of both triumph and hardship. The tight-knit community, the changing seasons, and the familiar faces were all part of a chapter that had shaped us. It was time for a fresh start, a new resolve to carry us into the next chapter of our lives.

Florida, with its warm climate and vibrant communities, promised a new beginning. The thought of living near the serene beaches, where the ocean waves could wash away the remnants of our past struggles, was both comforting and invigorating. It was a chance to rebuild, not just our lives, but our spirits.

Finding My Roots in Construction

My father, Frank Grage, had always been a pillar of strength and wisdom in my life. He had instilled in me a deep respect for hard work and the satisfaction of creating something with my own hands. As we settled into our new life in Florida, I found myself returning to my roots in construction. The knowledge and skills my father had imparted to me became the foundation upon which I began to rebuild our lives.

Construction, much like weightlifting and CrossFit, required dedication, precision, and strength. It was a craft that demanded both physical and mental resilience. As I immersed myself in this work, I found the same joy and fulfillment that I had once found in the gym and the ring. Each project was a new challenge, a new opportunity to create and build.

Rebuilding and Rediscovering Joy

The process of rebuilding was not just about physical structures but about rediscovering joy and purpose. The satisfaction of seeing a project come to life, from the initial plans to the final touches, reignited a passion within me. It was a reminder that, no matter how many times we fall, we have the strength to rise again and create something beautiful.

In this journey, I often reflected on a conversation between Bruce Wayne and his father in the updated Batman movies. Thomas Wayne asked, "Why do we fall, Bruce? So that we can learn to pick ourselves up." This reminded me that every fall is an opportunity to learn and grow stronger.

Working in construction also allowed me to connect with my father's legacy on a deeper level. Every truss I placed, every wall I built, was a tribute to the lessons he had taught me. It was a way to honor his memory and the values he had instilled in me. The physical labor, the meticulous planning, and the creativity involved in construction brought me a sense of peace and fulfillment.

Embracing a New Community

Moving to Florida also meant becoming part of a new community. Just as we had built a family at CFPB, we began to forge new relationships in our new home. The warmth and openness of the people we met were a balm to our weary souls. We found support and camaraderie among neighbors and fellow workers, creating new bonds that helped ease the transition. Even bringing Spanish linguistics to the kitchen.

The beaches became our sanctuary. The sound of the waves, the feel of the sand beneath our feet, and the stunning sunsets provided a sense of tranquility and hope. It was a reminder that life, much like the ocean, has its ebb and flow. There are times of turbulence, but also moments of calm and beauty.

Our family found new joys in outdoor activities like stand-up paddleboarding, paddle skateboarding, longboarding, and swimming. These activities not only kept us physically active but also brought us closer together. We may have even created a new fitness idea with paddle skateboarding, blending the skills of paddleboarding with the thrill of longboarding. These shared experiences became a foundation of our new life, filling our days with laughter, adventure, and a renewed sense of purpose.

Coach Ryan: The Warrior's Spirit

Coach Ryan, Coach Dad, Coach Ryan Rage – these identities all embody the relentless spirit that defines our journey. I've learned that you can't be afraid to act, to take the leap when necessary. Not everything will work out perfectly, and that's okay. You can't expect perfection. It's the willingness to jump and the courage to face whatever comes next that truly matters.

"All the heavens and all the hells are within you." This quote, from the famous movie **13 Hours**, is a powerful reminder – WE have the choice in how we perceive and address the challenges in life. It's on YOU, it always has been. Never give up and always remember, you are the master of your fate and the captain of your soul.

New Beginnings

In this new chapter, we found strength in our resilience and hope in new beginnings. The struggles we had faced were not forgotten, but they became part of our story, shaping us into who we are today. We embraced the opportunity to start fresh, to build a life filled with joy, purpose, and new possibilities.

My dear children and grandchildren, as you face your own journeys, remember that there is always a path to renewal. The challenges and struggles you encounter will shape you, but they do not define you. Find strength in your roots, honor the lessons of those who came before you, and never be afraid to start anew.

Conclusion: Embrace the Grind, Embrace the Future

Life is hard. It's a relentless grind, a never-ending series of battles that will test your resolve, your spirit, and your will to continue. But remember this: it's in those moments of struggle that you will find your true strength. The world will throw everything it has at you—failure, loss, betrayal—but you have the power to rise above it all.

Stay ready. Always be prepared for the next challenge. Train your mind, your body, and your spirit to be resilient, to adapt, and to overcome. The journey is never easy, but it's the hard paths that lead to the greatest destinations. As Epictetus said, "The greater the difficulty, the more glory in surmounting it. Skillful pilots gain their reputation from storms and tempests."

As Donald Trump once said, "Sometimes by losing a battle you find a new way to win the war." React with strength. React with determination. React with the unwavering belief that you can and will overcome.

Embrace the grind. Wake up every day with a hunger to improve, to push your limits, and to be better than you were yesterday. Find joy in the journey, not just the destination. Celebrate the small victories, learn from the defeats, and keep moving forward.

This is your legacy. This is your story. Write it with courage, resilience, and an unbreakable spirit. Never back down, never give up, and always remember that the power to shape your future lies within you.

With all my heart,
Ryan Grage (Coach Ryan Rage)

Final Conclusion

As the sun sets over the serene beaches of Sarasota, Florida, I reflect on the incredible journey that has brought me here. These are the tales of a journey forged through blood, sweat, and tears. From the fiery trials of my past to the triumphant highs of my athletic career, every step, every challenge has shaped me into the man I am today. My legacy, built on resilience, unwavering dedication, and the transformative power of fitness, now extends beyond personal achievements to touch the lives of countless others.

Surrounded by the love of my family, I know that the true measure of my success lies not in the medals and records, but in the lives I have changed. My children, a testament to my strength and love, grow each day under the guiding principles Amber and I instill in them—creativity, empathy, and a relentless drive to be their best selves.

If someone says I was a business owner who sought perfection, they are right. If someone says I was willing to call out the problem in the room, they are right. If someone says I wore my heart on my sleeve and was over the top at times, they might be right too. If they say I pushed every athlete I was given the honor to train, regardless of their age, size, or athletic ability, they would be correct. I intentionally pushed the limits for every individual, attempting to show them a portion of their true value. They paid me to do it, and I brought that energy to every class, every training session, and every open workout. My goal was to lead others to greatness and, in turn, be great together—to build the team up.

In the stillness of the evening, I feel the presence of those who have walked beside me on this journey. My Grandpa Weber, a rock in my youth, smiles down upon me, proud of the man who chose to stand for something different. The echoes of past hardships, from the loss of newborns to the struggles of my business, now serve as reminders of my incredible resilience. Amber's cancer scare after the birth of our miracle baby, Gunnar, was another trial that tested our strength and faith, yet only made us stronger and more united.

"Always on your left, always loving 4444," I whisper, the phrase now a mantra that embodies my unwavering support and boundless energy for those I care about. It's not just a signature; it's a promise—a commitment to be there, pushing, encouraging, and loving with all my might.

As the waves crash gently on the shore, I envision a future where my legacy of strength, compassion, and relentless perseverance continues to inspire. I know that while I have reached many summits, the journey is far from over. With each sunrise, a new chapter begins, filled with opportunities to lift others, to share wisdom, and to leave an indelible mark on the world.

My story, filled with epic triumphs and profound lessons, is a celebration of the power of the human spirit. And as the final page turns, I stand tall, ready to embrace whatever comes next with the same grit and grace that have defined my journey.

For in the end, it's not just about the battles fought or the victories won—it's about the lives touched, the hearts inspired, and the legacy of love and strength that will endure long after the last weight is lifted and the final bell rings.

To those who have walked away or lost touch, I hope you find the fire within to chase your dreams, to never settle, and to push beyond the limits you once believed insurmountable. To those who have stayed, who have fought alongside me, who have believed in the vision, your dedication fuels my soul. Our bond is unbreakable, our mission clear, and our path paved with the sweat and determination of those who dare to strive for greatness.

And now, I give you 11 weeks of workouts that were completed at CFPB as Amber and I attempted to qualify for the 2019 CrossFit Games. These workouts were the map that led us to greatness. I ended up 98th out of 35,000 in the world and Amber 204th out of 24,000. We were among the top in the world and the United States. There was never a fitter couple. I hope you enjoy the workout ideas, and when you finish, please begin writing your own workouts. Don't quit. Every day, do something that shows fitness is the model of life and success. #100dayfitnesschallenge.

To my family, my friends, and all who walk this path, may you remember the spirit of Ryan and Amber for millennia. Our journey, our struggles, and our triumphs are now part of a legacy that will live on through you. Keep pushing, keep striving, and never forget that greatness lies within each of you. Always here loving 4444.

In the end, it's the battles fought, the victories won, and the lives touched that define our true legacy. This is my story—a celebration of the unyielding power of the human spirit and a call to action for all who seek to carve their path. Stand tall, embrace the journey, and let your legacy be a beacon of strength, love, and unwavering resolve.

1. **Workout: "Freddy Krueger"**
Strength:
- Front Squat 1RM (One Rep Max)

Conditioning:
- **"Freddy Krueger" (21-15-9):**
  - KB Swings (70/55 lbs.)
  - Burpees (55/35 lbs.)

Average Time for All Participants: 16:05 minutes

---

2. **Workout: "Crash Course"**
15 MIN AMRAP (As Many Rounds As Possible):
- 27/18 Cal Bike
- 21 Sit-Ups
- 15 Chest to Bar Pull-Ups
- 10 DB Snatch (50/35 lbs.)

Average Rounds Completed by All Participants: 3.46 rounds

---

3. **Workout: "Joker"**
1-2-3-4-5-6-7-8-9-10 Toes to Bar
- 10-9-8-7-6-5-4-3-2-1 Deadlifts
  - Open: 225/155 lbs.
  - Perf: 185/135 lbs.
  - Fit: 155/105 lbs.

Average Time for All Participants: 11:53 minutes

---

4. **Workout: "Teams of 5!"**
30 MIN AMRAP (As Many Rounds As Possible):
- 8 DB Hang Clean and Jerk (50/35 lbs.)
- 8 DB Lunges (4 per leg, 50/35 lbs.)
- 12/18 Cal Bike

Average Rounds Completed by All Teams: 17.92 rounds

---

5. **Workout: "Happy X-mas Eve 2018!"**
- 70/50 Cal Row
- 60 Box Jumps (24/20 inches)
- 60 Burpees
- 50 KB Swings (53/35 lbs.)
- 50 Sit-Ups
- 40 DB Snatch (50/35 lbs.)
- 40 Lunges
- 30 HSPU or 50 Push-Ups
- 30 Thrusters (75/55 lbs.)

Average Time for All Participants: 34:39 minutes

NOTES:

6. **Workout: "Boxing Day"**

2 Rounds for Time:
- Double Unders
    - O (50)
    - P (40)
    - F (30)
- 25 Hang Cleans
    - O (95/65 lbs.)
    - P (75/55 lbs.)
    - F (65/45 lbs.)
- Double Unders
- 25 Push Press
- Double Unders
- 25 Bar Facing Burpee Bar Hops

Average Time for All Participants: 17:30 minutes

---

7. **Strength:**
- Overhead Squat: Heavy Set of 5

Conditioning:
- **12 Min AMRAP (As Many Rounds As Possible):**
    - 5 Strict HSPU
    - 10 Overhead Squats
        - O (95/65 lbs.)
        - P (75/55 lbs.)
        - F (65/45 lbs.)
    - 15 Deadlifts (same weight as OHS)

Average Rounds Completed by All Participants: 5.47 rounds

---

8. **Workout: "Vader"**

3 Rounds for Time:
- 24/17 Cal Row
- 21 Wall Balls
    - O (20/14 lbs.)
    - P (14/10 lbs.)
- 18 DB Snatch
    - O (50/35 lbs.)
    - P (35/20 lbs.)
- 15 Burpees over DB (lateral)

Average Time for All Participants: 17:18 minutes

NOTES:

9. Workout: "Partner Day"
35 MIN CAP:
- 1000/800 m Row
- 50 Toes to Bar
- 70/50 Cal Bike
- 50 Power Cleans
    - T (115 lbs.)
    - P (155/105 lbs.)
    - F (135/95 lbs.)
- 70/50 Cal Bike
- 50 Toes to Bar
- 1000/800 m Row

Average Time for All Participants: 26:21 minutes

---

10. Workout: "Happy New Year's Eve 2018!"
- 10 Bar Muscle-Ups, 20 CTB Pull-Ups, or 30 Jumping PU/Ring Rows
- 20 Slam Ball over Shoulder
- 30 DB Hang Clean and Jerk
- 40 Overhead Plate Lunges
- 50 Hand Release Push-Ups
- 50 Wall Balls
- 40 Sit-Ups
- 30 Burpee Box Jumps (24/20 inches)
- 20 Slam Ball over Shoulder
- 10 Bar Muscle-Ups, 20 CTB Pull-Ups, or 30 Jumping PU/Ring Rows

Average Time for All Participants: 29:54 minutes

---

11. Workout: "New Year's Team WOD"
Teams of 3 (45 Min CAP):
- 60/45 Cal Bike, 30 Clean and Jerks (95/65 lbs.)
- 60/45 Cal Row, 30 Clean and Jerks (115/80 lbs.)
- 60/45 Cal Bike, 30 Clean and Jerks (135/95 lbs.)
- 60/45 Cal Row, 30 Clean and Jerks (155/105 lbs.)
- 60/45 Cal Bike, 30 Clean and Jerks (165/115 lbs.)
- 60/45 Cal Row, 30 Clean and Jerks (185/135 lbs.)

Average Time for All Teams: 39:41 minutes

NOTES:

12. **Workout: "Copper Lung"**
Back Squat:
- On the 3:00, 3x10 across (65-75%)

Conditioning: "Copper Lung":
- **Cal Bike:**
    - o   Guys: 21-15-9
    - o   Ladies: 15-10-5
- 21-15-9 Russian KB Swings
    - o   O (70/55 lbs.)
    - o   P (55/35 lbs.)
- **Rest 3 minutes**
- **Cal Row:**
    - o   Guys: 21-15-9
    - o   Ladies: 15-10-5
- 21-15-9 Goblet Squats

Average Time for All Participants: 15:10 minutes

---

13. **Workout: "Stuffing Removal"**
5 Rounds for Time:
- 15 Burpees
- 25 Sit-Ups
- 50 Double Unders

Average Time for All Participants: 21:29 minutes

---

14. **Workout: "Over the Holidays"**
20 Min AMRAP (As Many Rounds As Possible):
- 5 Hang Power Snatch
    - o   O (95/65 lbs.)
    - o   P (75/55 lbs.)
    - o   F (45 lbs.)
- 10 Push-Ups
    - o   P/F: Hand Release Push-Ups
- 15 Air Squats
- 15/12 Cal Row

Average Rounds Completed by All Participants: 7.18 rounds

NOTES:

15. Workout: "Fran-tastic" or "Fran"
Fran-tastic:
- 21 Thrusters (115/80 lbs.)
- 9 Ring Muscle-Ups
- 15 Thrusters
- 15 Chest to Bar Pull-Ups
- 9 Thrusters
- 21 Pull-Ups

Fran:
- 21-15-9 Thrusters (95/65 lbs.)
- 21-15-9 Pull-Ups

Average Time for All Participants: 10:52 minutes

---

16. Workout: "Air Walker"
20 Min AMRAP (As Many Rounds As Possible):
- 25/18 Cal Row
- 50 Double Unders
- 3 Power Cleans
    - O (135 lbs.)
    - P (115 lbs.)
    - F (95 lbs.)
- 6 Push-Ups
- 9 Air Squats

Average Rounds Completed by All Participants: 6.02 rounds

---

17. Workout: "Front Squat and Snatch"
Front Squat
- 3x10 across @ 65-75% (On the 3:00, Complete 10 Reps)

Snatch
- Build to a Heavy Power Snatch

Average Weights for Front Squat:
- **Women:** 122 lbs.
- **Men:** 172 lbs.

Average Weights for Snatch:
- **Women:** 72 lbs.
- **Men:** 116 lbs.

NOTES:

18. Workout: "Clothesline"
12 Min AMRAP (As Many Rounds As Possible):
- Up Ladder by 2's (2, 4, 6, 8, 10, 12, etc.)
  - Push Press
    - O (115/80 lbs.)
    - P (95/65 lbs.)
    - F (75/55 lbs.)
  - Toes to Bar
  - Box Jump Overs
    - O (24/20 inches)
    - P/F (20/14 inches)

Average Rounds Completed by All Participants: 6.4 rounds

---

19. Workout: "Bee's Knees"
5 Rounds:
- 1 Min Wall Balls (20/14 lbs.)
- 1 Min KB Swings (55/35 lbs.)
- 1 Min Air Bike
- 1 Min Rest

Average Reps Completed by All Participants: 269 reps

---

20. Workout: "DT"
5 Rounds for Time:
- 12 Deadlifts (155 lbs.)
- 9 Hang Cleans (155 lbs.)
- 6 Push Jerks (155 lbs.)

Average Time for All Participants: 11:33 minutes

---

21. Back Squat
- 4x8 @ 75-78% (On the 2:45, 0:00, 2:45, 5:30, 8:15)

Conditioning: "Satan's Whiskers"
- 3 Rounds for Time:
  - 10 Front Squats (O: 155/105 lbs, P: 135/95 lbs, F: 105/75 lbs)
  - 10 Chest to Bar Pull-Ups (or Pull-Ups)
  - 10 Burpees

Average Time for All Participants: 10:34 minutes

NOTES:

22. Work It Wednesday: "The Cycle"

- Cal Row: 70/50
- Double Unders: O (100), P (75), F (50)
- 30 DB Snatches: O/P (50/35 lbs.), F (35/20 lbs.)
- Double Unders
- 30 DB Hang Clean + Jerks: O/P (50/35 lbs.), F (35/20 lbs.)
- Double Unders
- Cal Bike: 70/50

Average Time for All Participants: 22:45 minutes

---

23. Workout: "Do it Right"
25 Min AMRAP (As Many Rounds As Possible):

- 5 Strict Pull-Ups
- 10 Honest Push-Ups
- 15 Full Depth Air Squats
- 30 Ab Mat Sit-Ups
- 50' Med Ball Carry

Average Rounds Completed by All Participants: 6.7 rounds

---

24. Workout: "Task Priority FGB"
3 Rounds for Time:

- 30 Wall Balls O/P (20/14 lbs.), F (14/10 lbs.)
- 30 Box Jumps O/P (24/20 inches), F (20/14 inches)
- 30 Sumo Deadlift High Pulls: O/P (75/55 lbs.), F (45 lbs.)
- 30 Push Press: O/P (75/55 lbs.), F (45 lbs.)
- 30/21 Cal Row (Reference: 25 Reps of Fitness = 20 reps)
- Rest 2 minutes after each round

Average Time for All Participants: 29:21 minutes

---

25. Workout: "Teams of 3!"
2 Rounds (35 Min CAP):

- 30 Bar Facing Burpees
- 30 Hang Cleans (O: 135/95 lbs., P/F: 95 lbs.)
- 30 Toes to Bar
- 120/90 Cal Bike

Average Time for All Teams: 35:17 minutes

NOTES:

26. Workout: "Two Scoops"
3 Rounds for Time:
- 20 DB Snatch (O: 50/35 lbs., F: 35/20 lbs.)
- 50 Double Unders
- 20 DB Front Squat (O: 50/35 lbs., F: 35/20 lbs.)
- 50 Double Unders
- 20 Handstand Push-Ups (F: Hand Release Push-Ups)

Average Time for All Participants: 21:34 minutes

---

27. Workout: "Chain Reaction"
3 Rounds:
- 21/15 Cal Bike or Row
- 7 Pull-Ups
- 7 Toes to Bar
- 7 Chest to Bar Pull-Ups

Directly into 3 Rounds:
- 9 Power Cleans (O: 155/105 lbs., P: 135/95 lbs., F: 105/75 lbs.)
- 9 Shoulder to Overhead

Average Time for All Participants: 17:03 minutes

---

28. Workout: "Crack a Cold One"
   Build to a Heavy Power Snatch
   9 Min AMRAP (As Many Rounds As Possible):
- 3, 6, 9, 12, 15, 18, 21, continue up by 3's:
    - Deadlift (O: 225/155 lbs., P: 205/145 lbs., F: 185/135 lbs.)
    - Bar Facing Burpee Bar Hops

Average Rounds Completed by All Participants: 15 rounds

---

29. Workout: "Front Squat and Cashout"
Strength:
- Front Squat: 4x8 across @ 70-78%
- On the 2:45 (0:00, 2:45, 5:30, 8:15)

Cashout:
- 3 Rounds for Technique:
    - 10 Strict Toes to Bar or 20 Sit-Ups
    - 20 Weighted Lunges (DB/KB Farmer or Goblet)
    - 1 min plank / 45 sec HS hold

Average Weight for Front Squats:
- **Women:** 115.8 lbs.
- **Men:** 174.4 lbs.

NOTES:

30. Workout: "Partner Day AMRAP"
25 Min AMRAP:
- 50/40 Cal Row
- 40 Box Jump Overs (24/20)
- 30/20 Cal Bike
- 20 Ring Dips

Average Rounds Completed by All Participants: 3.78 rounds

---

31. Workout: "Partner Day Waterfall Style"
0:00 - 10:00 (Waterfall Style)
Up Ladder by 1's (1,2,3,4,5, etc.):
- Devil Press (50/35 lbs.)
- Bar Muscle Ups
- **Rest 3 Min**

13:00 - 33:00 (Waterfall Style):
- 10 DB Hang Clean and Jerk (50/35 lbs.)
- 10 DB Snatch (50/35 lbs.)
- 10 Chest to Bar Pull-Ups
- 15/12 Cal Bike

Average Rounds Completed by All Participants: 7.02 rounds

---

32. Workout: "Go Fish"
Push Press: 5x3 (Building in weight)
Conditioning: "Go Fish":
- 1000/800m Row
- Directly into 3 Rounds of:
  - 21 Deadlifts (O: 135/95 lbs., P: 115/80 lbs., F: 95/65 lbs.)
  - 15 Burpees
  - 9 Shoulder to Overhead

Average Time for All Participants: 12:44 minutes

NOTES:

33. Workout: "Layup"
Warm-up:
- 50-40-30-20-10
  - Double Unders
  - Sit-Ups

Directly into:
- 5-10-15-20-25
  - Kettlebell Swings (55/35)
  - Wall Balls (20/14)

Average Scores:
- **Men:** 19:12
- **Women:** 19:56

---

34. Strength:
- Back Squat 5x6 @ 75-82% of 1RM on the 2:30

Partner Day - AMRAP 25min:
- 10 Chest to Bar Pull-ups
- 14 Handstand Push-ups or Strict Push-ups
- 20 Pistols or Air Squats
- 10 Devil Presses (50/35)

Average Scores:
- **Men:** 10 rounds
- **Women:** 8 rounds

---

35. Workout: "Heat Wave"
20 Min AMRAP:
- 10 Bar Facing Burpees
- 10 Hang Cleans (115/80) (95/65) (75/55)
- 15/12 Cal Bike or Row

Average Scores:
- **Men:** 5 rounds
- **Women:** 4.5 rounds

---

36. Workout: "Hangnail"
16 Min AMRAP:
- 20 Dumbbell Hang Clean and Jerk (50/35) (35/20)
- 20/15 Cal Bike
- 15 Bar Facing Burpees
- 15 Deadlifts (245/165) (225/155) (205/145)

Average Scores:
- **Men:** 4.5 rounds
- **Women:** 4 rounds

NOTES:

37. Strength:

- Front Squat 5x6 across @ 75-82%

Conditioning: "Got Your Name On It"

- 8 Min AMRAP:
  - 8 Dumbbell Snatches (50/35) (35/20)
  - 30 Double Unders

Average Scores:

- **Men:** 7 rounds
- **Women:** 6 rounds

38. Workout: Partner Day - 25 Min AMRAP

25 Min AMRAP:

- 60 Wall Balls
- 50/40 Cal Row
- 40 Toes to Bar
- 30 Burpee Box Jump Overs (24/20)
- 20 Ring Muscle Ups

Average Scores:

- **Men:** 1,150 reps (combined)
- **Women:** 1,130 reps (combined)

39. Workout: Partner Day (35 Min CAP):

- 150 Double Unders
- 200 Sit-Ups
- 150 Double Unders
- 100 Hang Snatches (75/55) (45/35)
- 150 Double Unders
- 100 Pushups
- 150 Double Unders

Average Scores:

- **Men:** 27:52
- **Women:** 28:14

40. Strength:

- Back Squat 6x4 @ 82-90% of 1RM on the 2:15

Conditioning: "Simply Stunning" - 21-15-9

- Kettlebell Swings (70/53) (53/35)
- Burpee Box Jump Overs (24/20)

Average Scores:

- **Men:** 11:35
- **Women:** 12:10

NOTES:

41. Workout: "Elizoburpee"
21-15-9:
- Squat Cleans (135/95) (115/80) (95/65)
- Bar Facing Burpees

Average Scores:
- **Men:** 11:40
- **Women:** 12:20

---

42. Workout: "Soulmates" (25 Min CAP):
- 50/35 Cal Bike
- 20 Power Cleans (135/95) (115/80) (95/65)
- 40/30 Cal Row
- 15 Power Cleans (135/95) (115/80) (95/65)
- 30/21 Cal Bike
- 10 Power Cleans (155/105) (135/95) (115/80)
- 21/15 Cal Row
- 5 Power Cleans (185/135) (155/105) (135/95)

Average Scores:
- **Men:** 21:40
- **Women:** 22:15

---

43. Workout: "Main Page"
20 Min CAP:
- 5 Strict Pullups + 10 Pushups + 15 Squats
- 10 Strict Pullups + 20 Pushups + 30 Squats
- 20 Strict Pullups + 40 Pushups + 60 Squats
- 40 Strict Pullups + 70 Pushups + 120 Squats

Average Scores:
- **Men:** 250 reps
- **Women:** 230 reps

---

44. Workout: "The Last Fight"
20 Min AMRAP:
- 20 DB Snatch (50/35) (35/20)
- 20/15 Cal Row
- 20 Toes to Bar
- 20/15 Cal Bike

Average Scores:
- **Men:** 3 rounds + 35 reps
- **Women:** 3 rounds + 20 reps

NOTES:

BONUS WORKOUTS:

For Reps or Time (30 Min CAP):
- 60/40 Cal Row
- 50 Deadlifts (135/95)
- 40 Hang Cleans
- 30 Shoulder to OH

Average Scores:
- **Men:** 468
- **Women:** 362

Workout: Partner Day!
2 Rounds of the following:
- 3 Min AMRAP - air dyne
- 3 Min REST
- 3 Min AMRAP - Power Snatch (95/65)
- 3 Min REST
- 3 Min AMRAP - CTB Pullups
- 3 Min REST

Average Scores:
- **Men:** 374
- **Women:** 314

Workout: "Case Closed"
6 Rounds on the 4 Min:
- 12 DB Hang Clean + Jerk (50/35)
- 12 Burpees
- 12 10m Shuttle Sprints

Average Scores:
- **Men:** 2:05
- **Women:** 2:20

Workout: "Squeaky Wheels"
20 Min AMRAP:
- Double Unders (60)
- 20/15 Cal Row
- 20 Sit-ups
- 20/15 Cal Bike

Average Scores:
- **Men:** 377
- **Women:** 368

NOTES:

Workout: "Heavy Dose"
10 Min AMRAP:

- 9 Power Cleans (135/95, 115/80, 95/65)
- 7 Strict HSPU
- 5 Strict Pullups

Average Scores:

- **Men:** 5 rounds + 10 reps
- **Women:** 6 rounds + 5 reps

Workout: "Bloodshot Eyes"
5 Rds for Time:

- 250/200m Row
- 20 KBS (55/35)
- 20 Wallballs (20/14)
- 20 Box Jumps (24/20)

Average Scores:

- **Men:** 30:05
- **Women:** 28:45

Workout: "Open 19.1"
15 Min AMRAP:

- 19 Wall Balls (20/14)
- 19 Cal Row

Average Scores:

- **Men:** 7 rounds + 5 reps
- **Women:** 8 rounds

NOTES:

Workout: "Partner Day!" (35 Min CAP):
- 40/30 Cal Bike
- 50 Pull-ups
- 50 Push-ups
- 20 Clean & Jerks (135/95, 115/80, 95/65)
- 40/30 Cal Bike
- 40 Toes to Bar
- 40 Push-ups
- 20 Clean & Jerks (135/95, 115/80, 95/65)
- 40/30 Cal Bike
- 30 Bar Muscle Ups
- 30 Push-ups
- 20 Clean & Jerks (135/95, 115/80, 95/65)

Average Scores:
- **Men:** 34:30
- **Women:** 33:15

Strength:
- Back Squat 7x2 Across @90-95% on the 2:00

Conditioning: "This or That"
- 10 Min AMRAP:
    - 10 Toes to Bar
    - 10 DB Goblet Squats (50/35)
    - 10 DB Hang Clean & Jerks (50/35)

Average Scores:
- **Back Squat:** 205 lbs.
- **AMRAP rounds:** 5 rounds

NOTES:

Workout: "Face Off"
5 Rounds on the 4 Min:
- 9 Deadlifts (225/155)
- 12 Bar-facing burpees
- 15/12 Cal Bike

Average Scores:
- **Fastest time:** 2:58
- **Slowest time:** 3:48

Strength:
- Build to a Heavy Power Snatch

Conditioning: "Over It"
- 20-16-12-8:
  - Dual DB Box Step Ups (50/35)
  - Pull-ups
  - DB Snatch (Alternating)

Average Scores:
- **Power Snatch:** 145 lbs.
- **Time:** 14:56

Workout: "Annabelle"
50/35 Cal Bike
- 75 Double Unders
- 75 Sit-ups
- 40/25 Cal Bike
- 50 Double Unders
- 50 Sit-ups
- 35/20 Cal Bike
- 25 Double Unders
- 25 Sit-ups

Average Scores:
- **Time:** 21:38

NOTES:

Ode of Inspiration

Introduction

In the marvel multiverse of life, there are countless realities shaped by those who inspire us, guide us, and lift us when we are at our lowest. This final chapter is an ode to the remarkable individuals who have been my sources of strength, wisdom, and inspiration. Their impact on my life has been profound, and their legacies live on in the lessons they have imparted to me.

My Father, Frank Charles Grage

My journey begins with the man who taught me the value of hard work, integrity, and resilience—my father, Frank Charles Grage. Our relationship had its share of tumultuous moments, largely due to the strict religious upbringing that defined our family. I chose to leave that path, and though it created a rift between us for a time, we eventually rebuilt much of what was lost. Frank Charles Grage instilled in me a deep respect for hard work and the satisfaction of creating something with my own hands. He taught me everything I know about project management in construction, giving me the tools to succeed. Though I wish I had retained more of his wisdom and had more time to learn from him, his teachings remain invaluable. His wealth of knowledge is worth its weight in bitcoin and Ethereum, a treasure trove of skills and insights that have guided me throughout my life.

Lloyd Charles Grage

In stark contrast stands Lloyd Charles Grage, a figure whose presence in my life served as a lesson in what not to be. He was never a real grandfather to me. The only positive contribution he made to this world was passing on our strong DNA, resulting in the creation of my father. Beyond that, he left a legacy of absence and harsh lessons on the importance of being present and nurturing. I have not one good memory of him, nor do I care to try and understand his decisions in life. The darkness he brought into our family served as a stark reminder of the impact a father can have, both positive and negative. From Lloyd, I learned what it means to fail as a father and the importance of striving to be the opposite. With the thanks of a gentleman, I acknowledge his role in my lineage but reject his model of fatherhood.

Grandpa Weber, Bob Weber

Bob Weber, known affectionately as Grandpa Weber, was another towering figure in my life. He introduced me to the world of powerlifting and taught me the true meaning of inner strength. Under his guidance, I learned the hero mindset, the importance of never accepting failure, and the resilience needed to push through life's toughest challenges. My only regret is that I did not get to play football in high school. We tried every effort, and I even left home at 17 once trying to get on the team before my senior year. He also shared with me the joys of hunting, fishing, and living in the wilderness, fostering a deep appreciation for nature and self-reliance. His lessons on strength, both physical and mental, have been a cornerstone of my journey.

Tim Corey

Tim Corey was the first manager who took the time to grow me as a leader. At 19, he helped me get promoted to assistant manager and lead my own store for a short while, recruited by my brother from another mother, Matt Hughes. Tim was more than just a manager; he was a father figure who guided me with patience and wisdom. Tim's famous morning line was, "If you aren't 15 minutes early, you are late." That's how I live my life to this day because of his leadership. Through this career, I learned grit and the importance of perseverance. His belief in my potential and his willingness to mentor me during those formative years were instrumental in shaping my leadership skills and work ethic.

Uncle Bob

I always cherished my time with Uncle Bob. He taught me the importance of putting my arm around anyone in need, always answering the phone, and always having extra food on the grill because you never know who might show up. I loved the X-Men cartoon on Saturday mornings, a memory that always brings a smile to my face. His lessons in generosity and being there for others have shaped my approach to life and community.

My First-Born Son

Watching you grow into a man has been an incredibly rewarding journey. From the moment I held you, I knew my life had changed forever. Our drive together after your graduation from Iowa to Florida marked a significant chapter in your growth. The most crucial moment came when we were just minutes behind an accident—one that left multiple people dead. We were stopped on the highway, at a standstill for over two hours, in the dead of night. I saw the fear and uncertainty in your eyes. It was in that moment I witnessed a profound transformation. You were visibly shaken, but I could see you processing the gravity of life and death, grappling with the harsh realities of the world. In the stillness of that night, I saw you begin to turn from a boy into a man. Your growth, your strength, and your determination inspire me every day. You embody the values I hold dear, and I am incredibly proud of the man you are becoming. Keep pushing forward. Remember, you have the strength to overcome any obstacle.

My Daughter London

London, I have always felt a deep connection with you. You possess many of my characteristics and have a mother hen instinct, always taking care of the family when needed. You are the family protector and anchor when needed. We can communicate with just a look, understanding each other without words. Your strength and compassion are remarkable, and I am grateful for the bond we share. All my love, always.

My Daughter Makenna

Makenna, you will rule the world someday. Your determination and clarity about what you want are awe-inspiring. Raising a strong-willed child like you has been a challenge at times, but it is a challenge I cherish. I apologize for the days that were not great, but I thank you for all the positive and happy memories. I love being your dad and watching you navigate life with such confidence and resolve.

My Youngest Son Gunnar

Gunnar, you are our miracle baby, the youngest of my heirs and a source of daily joy and wonder. Becoming a dad again at 35 gave me a renewed perspective on life and parenting. You have taught me the importance of savoring every moment and have given me a glimpse of the joy I will share with my grandchildren. The energy and love you bring into my life are incomparable. You are my baby boy, and I am excited to see the man you will become.

My Boys, Hunter Clyde and Franklin Cash

To my boys who didn't make it to this world, Hunter Clyde and Franklin Cash, lost at 21 and 22 weeks. You lived into your early 20s of weeks of pregnancy, showing us the fragility and beauty of life. You were perfect little gems, and I hold you in my heart every day. Your memory drives me to succeed for our family. Though our time together was short, your impact on my life is eternal. Listen to "Smallest Wingless" by Craig Cardiff wherever you are.

My Wife, My Rock

To my wife, you are the rudder to my ship, the embodiment of Wonder Woman. You crush every role you take on and are my constant source of strength and support. The connection we share, especially during those soul-embracing hugs, is indescribable—it's straight fire. You didn't think this is all I would write about you, did you? I am working on our book, you know, The Notebook book. I don't know who will oversee reading it to whom, but I know that we will have the pages with all of the stories jotted down and ready to share. I don't know what my life would be without you. We are magnets, and I don't know if I can ever thank you enough for who you are in this legacy. Thank you, Mi Amor. I can never thank you enough for this life and for being my unwavering partner.

My Mom

Mom, I love you. I really do. I know that is enough for you to know that genuinely from my heart, I see you. I understand the struggles you went through growing up, the desire to escape the same issues I wanted out of. All my love, Mom.

Grandma Antoinette Grage

Grandma, you were the most important person in my life while growing up. Your care and concern for me taught me how to truly love another human being. I always felt loved by you, and I hope you knew that before your passing. Your legacy of love and kindness continues to guide me every day.

My Community

The members of CrossFit Port Byron (CFPB) have been a source of endless inspiration. They were not just clients; they were family. Everyone brought their unique strength, resilience, and spirit to our community. Together, we forged bonds that went beyond the gym walls, creating a support system that uplifted us all.

To the warriors who stood by me through thick and thin, your dedication and passion have been a constant source of motivation. Your stories of triumph over adversity, your unwavering commitment to personal growth, and your willingness to support one another have taught me the true meaning of community.

Philosophical Giants

The teachings of Marcus Aurelius, Seneca, and Epictetus have been my guiding light through the darkest of times. Their wisdom, encapsulated in stoic philosophy, provided a framework for understanding and overcoming life's challenges. Marcus Aurelius' reminder that "The impediment to action advances action. What stands in the way becomes the way," was a constant source of strength.

Seneca's teachings on resilience and acceptance of fate, and Epictetus' emphasis on focusing on what we can control, have been invaluable. Their words have shaped my approach to life, helping me navigate the storms with a calm and focused mind. The lessons they imparted are not just philosophical musings but practical tools for living a life of purpose and integrity.

Ryan Holiday

Dear modern stoic, your early books *The Obstacle is the Way* and *Courage is Calling* were monumental. However, I no longer hold you on a high pedestal after your recent books have slid politically so far left, they go against the teachings you once spoke of. I cannot even get through your latest book, *Do the Right Thing Right Now,* as it is so full of political jargon. You took a market share approach to your teachings. I hope to one day chat in person to better understand your current logic.

Matt Hughes

My brother that helped me survive my teenage years.

Modern-Day Warriors

In my journey, I have also been inspired by contemporary figures who embody the spirit of resilience and determination. David Goggins, with his relentless pursuit of self-mastery, taught me that the only limits we have are the ones we place on ourselves. His mantra of "Stay hard" resonates deeply with me, reminding me to push through pain and adversity.

Eric Thomas, the Hip-Hop Preacher, has been a source of daily motivation. In one of his videos, he recounts an Emmitt Smith commercial after he had JUST won the Super Bowl. Smith said, "I think I'm gonna rest now", as he rested for just 2-3 seconds while reppin out 225. This commercial reminds us that success is about continuous effort, never letting up even for a moment. His resilience in the face of hardship pulls at the heartstrings and reminds us of the incredible strength of the human spirit.

Conclusion

As I pen these final words, I am filled with a profound sense of gratitude. To those who have inspired me, guided me, and stood by me, thank you. Your influence has been immeasurable, and your impact on my life, everlasting. This journey, with all its trials and triumphs, has been a testament to the power of inspiration and the strength of the human spirit.

May we all strive to be sources of inspiration for others, to lift each other up, and to leave a legacy of strength, resilience, and love. This, my dear children and grandchildren, is the greatest lesson I can impart to you. Be inspired, and in turn, be an inspiration to others.

With all my heart,
Ryan Charles Grage

Made in the USA
Columbia, SC
16 September 2024

43f8e6a9-a96f-46a7-b1ad-61ee50c8749aR02